"Jason Fischer has an extra-ordinary thesis that to have an extra-ordinary relationship you have to know and apply the two truths about love, which are 'give permission' and 'take responsibility.' This is elegant and simple, and from my perspective and experience, true. I highly recommend *The Two Truths About Love* to everyone, therapists and couples."

—Harville Hendrix, PhD, author of *Getting the Love You Want*

"Simple yet not simplistic, the teachings in this book are wise and trustworthy riverbanks for the flow of intimate relationships."

—Tara Brach, PhD, author of *Radical Acceptance* and *True Refuge*

"To make something complicated is easy. To make it simple is much harder. And to be truly clear about what makes relationships extraordinary is elegant. This is what Jason Fischer and Sabrina Kindell have done in unfolding the two truths about relationships. In simple and accessible language, drawn from the lives of struggling couples, and supported by years of experience, both in the consulting room and on the meditation cushion, they have carefully offered the heart of the Buddha's wisdom woven intimately with insights from contemporary psychotherapy. The truths may look simple, but they clearly point to the fact that our relationships are, in fact, profound and enduring spiritual practices."

—Flint Sparks, PhD, psychologist and Zen priest, and resident teacher at Appamada, a center for Zen Practice and inquiry in Austin, TX

"The significance of relationships is present from the beginning of life, and continues to be a vital element in a lifetime of growth and development. This book makes a special contribution by defining the extraordinary relationship and pointing out some key elements in its development. I'm especially grateful to Jason Fischer and Sabrina Kindell for the clarity with which they lead us through the development of extraordinary relationships."

—LaNelle Brigance Ford, PsyD, author of *Overcoming Depression*

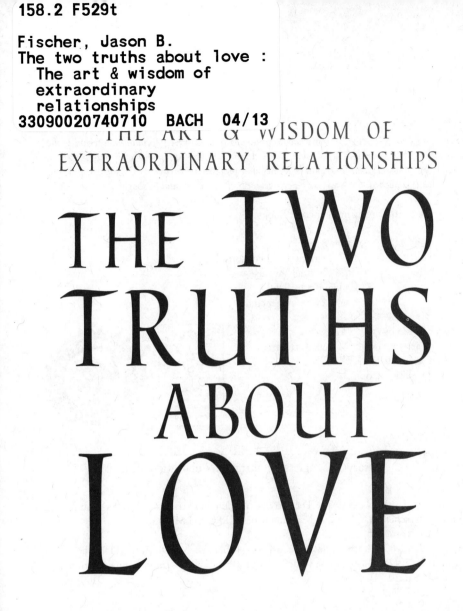

THE ART & WISDOM OF

EXTRAORDINARY RELATIONSHIPS

THE TWO
TRUTHS
ABOUT
LOVE

JASON B. FISCHER, MA, LPC

WITH SABRINA KINDELL, MA, LPC, LMFT

NEW HARBINGER PUBLICATIONS, INC.

Publisher's Note

This publication is designed to provide accurate and authoritative information in regard to the subject matter covered. It is sold with the understanding that the publisher is not engaged in rendering psychological, financial, legal, or other professional services. If expert assistance or counseling is needed, the services of a competent professional should be sought.

Distributed in Canada by Raincoast Books

Copyright © 2012 by Jason B. Fischer
New Harbinger Publications, Inc.
5674 Shattuck Avenue
Oakland, CA 94609
www.newharbinger.com

Cover design by Amy Shoup
Text design by Michele Waters-Kermes
Acquired by Melissa Kirk
Edited by Jasmine Star

Library of Congress Cataloging in Publication Data

Fischer, Jason B.
  The Two Truths about Love : The Art and Wisdom of Extraordinary Relationships / Jason B. Fischer, MA, LPC, and Sabrina Kindell, LPC-S, LMFT-S.
    pages cm
  ISBN 978-1-60882-516-5 (pbk. : alk. paper) -- ISBN 978-1-60882-517-2 (PDF e-book) (print) -- ISBN 978-1-60882-518-9 (ePub) (print) 1. Love. 2. Interpersonal relations. I. Kindell, Sabrina. II. Title.
  BF575.L8F57 2013
  158.2--dc23

                    2012029443

Printed in the United States of America

14   13   12

10   9   8   7   6   5   4   3   2   1   First printing

To Sunny and Xavier,
the loves of my life

Enlightenment is intimacy with all things.

—Zen master Dogen

CONTENTS

ACKNOWLEDGMENTS

A book, in many ways, is like a child. And, just as it takes a village to raise a child, so too does it take a village to raise an idea into a book. I am indebted to the many members of my village who contributed to raising this child.

Melissa Kirk I thank first for adopting this orphan book upon a single glance. I also thank the many folks at New Harbinger Publications who, working beside her, each had a hand in nurturing this child to adulthood, as well as Jasmine Star, editor extraordinaire. Peter Steinberg I thank for seeing the worth in this project and grabbing his bullhorn to tell others about it. Jinsoo Kim and Dorian Lucas I thank for being exactly as they are and for showing me the true nature of extraordinary friendship. I thank my family for a lifetime of ceaseless love, support, and influence, and, of course, I thank my wife for patiently and permissively walking the many steps of this journey with me.

Without Sabrina Kindell's assistance, unwavering compassion, mindful wisdom, and the inspiration our collaboration provided, I would have remained unable to convey my ideas nearly as comprehensibly. I thank her for the second wind she gave me in the eleventh hour of completing this book and look forward to working together for many years to come.

Special thanks go to Cindy Valero for her dedication and countless sacrifices in running Plumeria Counseling Center, as well as to my fellow therapists for sharing a vision and growing with me. To the many mentors who have shaped and inspired me along the way, I offer my inexhaustible gratitude—specifically Federico Mora, Jonathan Best, Phil Wagoner, Peter Mark, Ann-Ping Chin, Bong

Dal Kim, Bill Woodburn, Vagdevi Meunier, Gregg Unterberger, Bill Bruzy, and, yes, Sabrina.

Among my many instructors, above all I thank my clients, each and every one. Indeed, no one has shaped my abilities as a therapist and my philosophies about psychology and the human experience more than my clients. I owe my clients everything. And as often as I receive expressions of gratitude from those I am lucky enough to work with, the far greater gratitude is mine toward them. Those I teach are my teachers. I thank them all for the clarity they have bestowed upon me. What I know now I learned from them. This book could not exist without the many individuals and couples who have shared their hearts, minds, and time with me. Because of them, I am able to dedicate my life to passing along the lessons they've taught me.

—Jason B. Fischer, MA, LPC

Sometimes an adventure comes along that cannot be missed. Helping bring this book to life has been one such amazing journey. I want to offer a wholehearted thank-you to Jason Fischer, who entrusted me with his innovative concepts and keen understanding of what makes relationships work. When I started reading his manuscript, I had a hard time putting it down, which, truth be told, is uncommon for me after being in the field of relationship transformation and wellness for two decades. When I voiced my enthusiasm and feedback to Jason, he offered me the opportunity to assist him with the final push in crafting this book. Together, we spent many lively hours honing the core ideas into their current form. Jason's openness, authenticity, wisdom, compassion, and zest for living made it a joy to contribute to this worthwhile endeavor. His heart and soul are threaded throughout its pages, and I am grateful to have played a role, placing my spirit in the background and cheering him on.

I also want to acknowledge and thank my loving and supportive husband of twenty-five years, Brian, who from behind the scenes helped keep my spirits up and my heart ever full. I also extend a loving hug and big thanks to my children: my daughter, Brianna, who designed the graphics for this book, and whose kindness, creativity, skill, and brilliance fill me with delight; and my son, Alex, for his deep and loving understanding on those many afternoons when he came home from school to find me in front of the computer, where I sometimes remained late into the night. I extend a special and loving thanks to my father, Bob, and to my mother, River Cecilia, for being her beautiful self and listening with such love, pride, and presence to my joy about being a part of this project.

In addition I want to thank all those who have been integral in teaching me about extraordinary relationships: clients, interns, colleagues, friends, family, and all those who have touched my life along the way. May we all make it our mission to surround ourselves with extraordinary relationships wherever we go. Finally, I want to thank the readers of this book for choosing to be a part of this solution that can lead us all closer to love.

—Sabrina Kindell, LPC-S, LMFT-S
Contributing author and "book midwife"
www.counselingforlife.org

INTRODUCTION

Congratulations! You're about to embark on an amazing adventure. I'm excited for you, the way I feel excited whenever a new client walks into my office the first time. I'm excited because I know what you are about to learn and can anticipate the effect it will have on you and your relationships. I'm excited because I know the possibilities it offers. I'm excited because I know that, with the right tools, you can create the life and love you've always desired.

Because people often equate "love" with romantic relationships, that's the primary type of relationship this book addresses. However, the two truths about love are universal, and any type of relationship will benefit if you apply the approach and skills in this book to your interactions. For that reason, this book sometimes uses examples of other types of relationships or addresses relationships in general. That said, partner relationships can be among the most challenging, while also having the potential to be the most rewarding and extraordinary, so you may be highly motivated to apply these principles to romantic relationships. Chances are, after you experience the benefits of this approach in any relationship, you'll probably want to extend it to everyone you interact with.

You may wonder, *What is love? And how can there be only two truths about it?* Great questions! Love very well may be the most extraordinary emotional ability that we humans possess, and I'm fairly certain that our capacity to love is what most distinguishes us from all other species on the planet. Love is, indeed, extraordinary. It's also an emboldening characteristic of extraordinary relationships. As such, the two truths about love are also the two truths about extraordinary relationships. These two principles can enable all of us to cultivate extraordinary relationships, not just with others, but with ourselves and every aspect of the world around us.

You're also probably wondering, *What are these two truths?* They are the art of giving permission and the wisdom of taking responsibility. These are the two truths about love—and the two truths about joyfulness, harmony, intimacy, and peace. These two truths are akin to the Fourth Noble Truth of Buddhism: the path leading to the cessation of suffering. Although this is not a Buddhist book and I do not consider myself a Buddhist (despite having once been an ordained Buddhist monk), the ambition of this book is the same: to offer you a method for liberating yourself from suffering, allowing you to live an extraordinary life filled with extraordinary relationships. Learning and practicing the two truths explored in this book will help you forge your path. Since you may not entirely trust this yet, let me share a quick example.

I recently received a call from a client I had seen for only two sessions. She excitedly announced, "This philosophy of yours really works!" She then told me that she had just gotten off the phone with her husband, with whom she'd historically had a strained and conflict-ridden relationship. They were currently in a trial separation. She explained how, during their conversation, she had applied the principles we'd discussed in counseling, and then she told me, "You'll never guess what happened. Not a minute after hanging up, he sent me a text that said, 'I love you and I want to give our marriage another chance.' I started bawling when I read that. It was the first time in such a long time that he's said something like that to me. And it's exactly what I've been wanting to hear from him for ages!" This true story is just one of many similar tales.

When I first started my career as a therapist, I quickly learned that people want to work with someone who will do more than listen, nod, and ask how certain events in their lives make them feel. People want help. They want real answers, real solutions, real tools. They want insight into the difficulties they're experiencing and guidance on how to remedy them—not just for the moment, but for the rest of their lives. They want transformation.

If you're anything like the people I have the honor of working with in my counseling practice, you've come to a point where you recognize that some aspect of your life isn't quite the way you want it to be. You aspire toward change and aren't too proud to ask for a little help or guidance. That's precisely the type of person for whom this book is written.

This book is my way of welcoming you into my office and sharing a philosophy that works astoundingly well to transform suffering and cultivate extraordinary relationships. I know this philosophy works because I've seen it work, time and time again. In fact, I have yet to meet a person for whom it hasn't worked. That's why I'm confident that it can work for you too.

Many of my clients are shocked, at least initially, by much of what I have to say in therapy. "This is different," they tell me. They're right. This *is* different. I may reply, "This room isn't a place for normal thinking. You know normal thinking well enough already. What you don't know is something different than what you've been taught up until now. I see our time together as an opportunity to offer you something entirely new."

Have you ever met someone for the first time and then, only a few moments later, felt the person was profoundly familiar, as though you had known that person for years? Something similar is probably going to happen when you read this book. Although this philosophy will probably be completely foreign at first, it will quickly seem familiar, like something you've known all along. You might even wonder, *This is such common sense! Did I really just learn this?* Such is the beauty inherent in the simplicity of this philosophy: it's based on ideas that, after you experience them for yourself, will seem obvious.

You may be curious about where this philosophy came from. As a novice therapist, I knew I didn't have all the answers. Embracing this, I approached my counseling practice with the curiosity of an archaeologist, seeking to investigate and, from each unearthed shard, discover a bit more—more about human beings, more about what causes suffering, and, most importantly, more about what can be done to alleviate the suffering that afflicts so many of us, individually and in our relationships. I didn't want to simply lean on the theories of my predecessors; I wanted to learn for myself, from my own experience and observations. So as I met with each client, I listened for clues, kept an open mind, and strived to formulate my own understanding. As I did this, I kept a small journal beside my chair and scrawled quick notes to myself as bits of insight became evident to me. Piece by piece, the puzzle fell into place until one afternoon, thousands of counseling sessions later, it all came together as plain as day: the understanding I had been seeking.

In the years since, I have used the philosophy I developed over the course of that discovery process—the philosophy that's shared in this book. Its effects never cease to astound me, regardless of the number of times I witness its results. Along the way, many clients have urged me to put my philosophy in writing so it could be shared with others. Seeing the merits of doing so, I decided to give it a try. *But where to start*, I wondered, *when there is so much to say?*

I started with my journals, those many small notebooks I've been writing in since my first day as a therapist. I revisited each page and circled the most salient things I had written, and then built this book by elaborating on those points. Because of this, you'll find that most of the chapters are titled with a quote—a particular discovery that appeared in conversation with a client and subsequently proved meaningful for many other clients.

If you and I were to work together, in person, these ideas are much of what I would have to share with you. Now that you and I are together in this alternate way, let's not delay a minute longer when the path toward cultivating extraordinary relationships awaits within these pages. Thank you for sharing this time with me and opening your mind to discovering a new way of being and loving. As Zen master Shunryu Suzuki Roshi once said, "It is wisdom that is seeking wisdom."

I thank you for your wisdom.

PART 1

TOWARD THE
EXTRAORDINARY

1.
"EVERYTHING BOILS DOWN TO RELATIONSHIPS."

Relationships are at the very heart of human experience. We are all constantly relating: with partners or lovers, family members, pets, strangers, and friends; at work or school; with every aspect of our environment—the weather, traffic, current events, our finances, and so on; and with ourselves, our regrets or resentments about the past, our hopes or dreams for the future, and our dissatisfactions, both small and large, about our current situation, who we are or are not, and what we have or don't have. From this complex matrix of interwoven relationships, the entirety of our suffering and joy arises.

Whenever you suffer, whether alone or with others, the truth is always this: you are suffering due to an issue in one or more relationships. Maybe you don't know how to interact well with your partner or another loved one, or maybe you're struggling in your relationship with yourself, your life, or the world around you. Whatever the case, it always boils down to relationships and the solution is always the same: changing how you are relating.

As such, this book is not just about improving your relationships with others; it's about improving your ability to relate with *everything*, including yourself. By embracing a fresh paradigm for viewing relationships and learning new and effective tools for relating, you can transform suffering and skillfully build the extraordinary relationships you've always desired. This is what is possible once you discover the two truths about love.

2.
LOVE + ABILITIES = EXTRAORDINARY RELATIONSHIPS

Sure, love is grand. But successful relationships require more than just love. Unfortunately, love is not enough. What is? Love *plus* abilities. Only with effective abilities can you love in a way that is extraordinary.

When the state of a relationship is in disarray, when you are in major or minor conflict with another person, including inner conflict, you may understand only that you are suffering. You know you want love and peace in your relationships, whether with a romantic partner, family member, or close friend, and you also know that you don't want to suffer. Can you have it both ways? Can you love without suffering? The answer is yes, you can.

Contrary to how things may seem, love itself does not cause suffering. What does? Although this may be a radical notion, what typically causes suffering is the relationship abilities we've learned from others since childhood. These skills may have worked for a time, but at some point you probably started to notice that they don't work as well as you'd like. In fact, perhaps they mostly lead to conflict and disharmony. And although they are considered the normal or typical way of engaging in relationships, they don't effectively nurture the harmony and intimacy you likely desire.

By developing new abilities that will allow your relationships to flourish, you can increase your capacity to love without suffering. Indeed, you can learn how to approach your relationships in a way that is extraordinary.

For the purposes of this book, let's define "extraordinary" as "beyond the ordinary." This is exactly what this book offers: the skillful and sometimes revolutionary means and innovative tools it takes to relate to others, and yourself, in ways that are beyond the ordinary—in ways that foster a lasting experience of harmony and intimacy.

Although it is ordinary to suffer, you are not obligated to live and love in an ordinary way. You can opt for something different. You can dare to live extraordinarily instead, to cultivate extraordinary relationships that minimize both your own suffering and that of others. As such, this is precisely the invitation I extend to you now: to embrace the possibility that regularly practicing the abilities outlined in this book will allow you and your relationships to become "beyond the ordinary."

What this book offers is a powerful system for transforming suffering, achieving emotional wellness, and building an abundance of rewarding relationships. One of the best things about this system is how simple it is. In fact, the whole process centers around two abilities. That's it—just two: giving permission and taking responsibility. Think of these as the true "give and take" of relationships. You can give permission and take responsibility, at all times, with all people, and in all situations. This is the path of give-and-take that moves you toward developing extraordinary relationships. Over the course of this book, you are going to learn how to become a master at these two skills.

3.

"You don't find the right person: you become the right person."

Many people spend years searching for the right person with whom to share their life. If one relationship falters, the search continues. The longer this search persists, the more likely people are to grow despondent, wondering, *When will I find love?*

Most of us have been taught to approach relationships like shopping for a pair of shoes: We try on a pair to see how it fits. If it feels uncomfortable, we look for something that fits better. Unfortunately, this can result in walking around barefoot for a long time, perhaps growing increasingly calloused along the way.

In relationships, what starts out feeling comfortable tends to grow uncomfortable over time. Think about it: How many of your past romances began with blissful feelings? Each time, you might have thought, *At last, I've found my soul mate!* Then what happened? Conflicts may have begun to arise more often. Slowly, you probably lost touch with those first feelings and started to think, *Perhaps this isn't the right person after all.*

In truth, none of us is ever looking for the right person; we're looking for the right relationship. We're looking for a relationship that feels the way we want it to feel and feels that way enduringly, without growing uncomfortable or falling apart. The real question is not how to find the right person, but how to find the right relationship. How can you do that? By becoming the right person yourself.

4.

"YOU HAVE 99 PERCENT CONTROL OF EVERY RELATIONSHIP."

You've probably been taught that relationships are a fifty-fifty proposition—that for a relationship to work, it takes effort on the part of both people. I'll dare to suggest that this isn't true. Relationships actually don't require teamwork. In fact, you individually have the power to cultivate the life and relationships you desire, all by yourself.

Some of my greatest successes in therapy have been in working with people who sought counseling to improve a relationship. Usually their partner has refused to engage in therapy, so these clients come alone. I don't view this as a problem; actually, I love it, because I know that 99 percent of the time, it takes effort on the part of only one person for relationships to evolve in astounding ways, the exception being when someone completely refuses to participate in the relationship on any level.

When you understand that you possess 99 percent of the ability to transform your relationships, you put power where it can do the most good: in your own hands. When you embrace this, you can really start getting somewhere. This process is about what you yourself can change: how you can think differently, feel differently, speak differently, and act differently. The truth is, it takes only one to tango. When you want to dance, you can take the initiative to begin the dance all on your own.

5.

"A RELATIONSHIP IS AS STRONG AS ITS STRONGEST LINK."

You're probably familiar with the adage that a chain is only as strong as its weakest link. But when it comes to relationships, the opposite is true: every relationship is as strong as its *strongest* link. Even if the people you relate with don't join you on this journey, you can still create extraordinary relationships with them. How? By focusing on your willingness to consistently be the strongest link.

This process of growth and change is a path you travel as an individual. By focusing on yourself, you can discover, practice, and then ultimately master new ways of thinking, feeling, speaking, and being that are in keeping with your goals for personal fulfillment and creating loving connections with others. You have the power to be joyful, to create a life of your choosing, and to cultivate extraordinary relationships—with your partner, with others, with yourself, and with the world in general. Commit to becoming the strongest link in any and all of your relationships. As you strengthen as an individual, every connection you share with others will improve.

This is the amazing power you have to make a difference not only in your own life, but in the lives of all those you encounter. You start a chain reaction. When you relate to others differently, they relate to others differently, on and on, until all of humanity has been influenced—toward greater joy and togetherness—by the changes you have made. In this way, you are not just part of the solution; you are the entire solution. And it all starts right here, with you.

6.

"YOUR JOY IS YOUR JOB (AND NO ONE ELSE'S)."

I am never reminded of how in love with my wife I am more than when I look over at her and see her beaming with joy. She may be folding laundry, talking on the phone with a friend, or rocking our son to sleep. No matter what she's doing, if I see that she's joyful, I experience our relationship, at least in that moment, as existing in a blissful state of harmony and connectedness. This is the power of joyfulness.

When we are joyful, it's easier to view others with feelings of warmth and affection because we aren't distracted by our own suffering. When you're content, you can best savor others in a genuinely appreciative way. Similarly, when others are joyful, they emanate a beauty that is hard to ignore and hard not to admire. When you have made your own joy your job, then when others are similarly joyful it's fairly easy to share an extraordinary relationship.

A relationship between two genuinely joyful individuals is always going to be an extraordinary relationship—always. And, naturally, you can do a whole lot more about yourself than you can about others. This is why creating your joy is your job. Although at first it may seem selfish, nothing could be farther from the truth.

By cultivating your own joy, you accomplish two things: First, you experience a greater sense of ease and satisfaction with life. Second, others get to experience this as well, through their interactions with you. In this way, being joyful is actually an act of generosity, freeing others from trying to do this job for you. Besides, when another person tries to "make you" joyful, it very well may not work, and when it doesn't, the other person might feel inadequate or you might deem the person inadequate, which can put a major strain on the relationship. Therefore, making your joy your job is actually an act of compassion, as well. In fact, experiencing and expressing your personal sense of joy may be the greatest way of extending compassion to others.

Focusing on your own joyfulness doesn't mean becoming indifferent to the joy of others. You are absolutely entitled to want others to be joyful. The key is to recognize that the way to enable their joy is by taking responsibility for your own joy. After all, the more joyful you are, the more effectively you can nurture and support others in their pursuit of joyfulness. You can't do the work for them, but you can open the door.

But what does it mean to be joyful? You don't necessarily have to have a smile on your face to be joyful. Joy comes from within; it's a sense of serenity and fulfillment with life as it is, in all its manifold forms. For the purposes of this book, let's define joyfulness as any emotional state that occurs in the absence of suffering. As you decrease your suffering, you increase your joyfulness. As such, joyfulness is less about happiness and more about the transformation of suffering. The less you suffer, the more joyful you will be. The more joyful you are, the more joyful and extraordinary your relationships will be.

The process of cultivating extraordinary relationships begins with learning how to transform suffering in a skillful way. You can learn how to transform your own suffering and how best to serve others as they transform theirs. This is the starting point.

7.
"SUFFERING IS OPTIONAL."

As a result of life's challenges, many people may arrive at a conclusion that suffering is inevitable. In a way, this is true. If we look around us, we do indeed see much suffering. If you look at yourself, you probably see suffering there too. Maybe you feel that you're not as fulfilled or happy as you could be. Perhaps your relationship with your partner, a friend, or a particular loved one isn't exactly how you want, and perhaps you sometimes find yourself in conflicts that seem pointless and unnecessary. You may have a sense that something better is possible.

There's no question that humans suffer, some more than others. What accounts for the differences in the ways and degrees to which individuals suffer? What is suffering? Where does it truly come from? How can suffering be transformed? How can you create more joyfulness in your life? How can you cultivate harmonious and intimate relationships? You'll find the answers to these questions as you read on.

Suffering is not an inherent aspect of life. If it were, then all living things would suffer. Dragonflies would suffer, mosquitoes would suffer, grass would suffer, ferns would suffer. Clearly, suffering isn't inevitable in life. True, we humans suffer quite often, but it need not be this way. We can transform our suffering.

There's a Zen story about a young warrior who is mysteriously shot in the shoulder by an arrow while out in the woods hunting. In great pain, he looks for help in all directions. Finding a cool spring, he rinses his shoulder in the water. He then swiftly and with great effort removes the arrow. Then he begins to berate himself, calling himself names for hunting so late in the day and going alone. He rues his misfortune and concludes that he will never amount to a fine hunter. His self-judgments go on and on. It is as if he has shot himself with a second arrow—an arrow of his own making that only proliferates his suffering. What if instead he dressed his wound with a papaya leaf and headed back to the village to get it looked at, lesson learned, and that was that?

Whether afflicted by being alone on Valentine's Day, having recently gained a bit of extra weight, or contracting a chronic illness, we all have the opportunity to remove the second arrow, which is self-created and far more lethal—the arrow that is truly causing us to suffer. When we do this, we witness just how optional most of our suffering is.

Knowing that we don't want to suffer is helpful, but it isn't as helpful as knowing what we *do* want. What do we want? Most of us want the same thing: to feel joyful and get along well with others. In short, we want to exist and coexist in a satisfying way. The truth is, we all want this. In fact, three important things are true for all of us: We have a *right* not to suffer. We have a *desire* not to suffer. And we have the *ability* not to suffer. Yes, this applies to you too. You have the ability to be joyful, to create a life of your choosing, and to cultivate extraordinary relationships with others, yourself, and the world in general. In fact, you've always had this ability. You just haven't been shown how to fully tap into it. This book will help you do just that.

8.

"SUFFERING IS EMOTIONAL REACTIONS OUTSIDE YOUR COMFORT ZONE."

How do you know when you're suffering? When you are irritated or frustrated, angry or depressed, anxious or impatient, what tells you this is so? Simply put, you *feel* it. As such, let's define "suffering" as feeling a way that you do not, in a particular moment, want to be feeling. This is not to be confused with sadness, since you can be comfortable within a feeling of sorrow, especially when you recognize some sadness as a normal and appropriate part of your human experience.

We are all in a constant state of emotional flux, always responding to the world around us. Most of the time, our emotions maintain a healthy homeostasis within a normal range of emotional experience. Our emotions are always changing, but generally within a range wherein, for the most part, we feel fine and in control of ourselves. I call this range "the emotional comfort zone."

On a daily basis, you experience many emotions, mostly within the comfort zone: not so pronounced that you feel uncomfortable. While within this range, you remain in a state of calm. When I say "calm," I don't mean a flat-line experience of Zen-like satori or meditative bliss; I mean functioning within the comfort of a normal range of emotions. Throughout most of your life, therefore, you probably feel fairly calm, despite the fact that your emotions are ceaselessly fluctuating to some degree.

Every once in a while, however, an event occurs and you find yourself outside your comfort zone. Now you suddenly feel a way that you don't want to be feeling—an uncomfortable emotional state. Let's refer to these moments as "emotional reactions." While experiencing an emotional reaction, you are suffering a small or large degree of emotional pain. The further outside the comfort zone your emotion travels, the more discomfort you feel.

By this definition, when you experience an emotional reaction, you are suffering. And when you aren't experiencing an emotional reaction, you aren't suffering. Look at the diagram below to help you visualize this phenomenon.

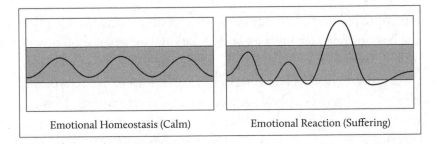

Emotional Homeostasis (Calm)   Emotional Reaction (Suffering)

The shaded area is your emotional comfort zone, while the rising and falling line represents your emotion, continuously morphing throughout time. On the left, your emotion remains within your comfort zone, so you feel calm. On the right, as your emotion extends beyond your zone, you suffer. When above your zone, you may feel anger, frustration, impatience, irritation, angst—states with an excess of emotional energy. When below, you may feel things like despair, despondency, and hopelessness—states in which energy is lacking. Whether above or below your zone, you are suffering.

If you are to better understand the nature of your suffering, it is vital to understand the nature of your emotional reactions. By working with your emotional reactions in a new way, you can learn how to transform your suffering in a new way. This involves a shift of focus from understanding *suffering* to understanding *emotional reactions*. Yet the two are actually one and the same.

Remember, suffering is emotional reaction, and emotional reaction is suffering. Whenever you're suffering, your emotion is outside your comfort zone. To stop suffering, merely return to your emotional comfort zone. Soon, I'll explain how.

9.

"EMOTIONAL REACTIONS ARISE FROM WITHIN."

An entire lifetime of conditioning has probably trained you to place the responsibility for much of your emotional experience on others, and to likewise take an excess of responsibility for the emotions of those around you. That this is the right way to be is typically ingrained through countless interactions with parents, siblings, friends, teachers, cohorts, colleagues, and even strangers. This perspective is often so embedded that it simply seems obviously true and valid. Consider these all-too-common types of statements:

- "You hurt my feelings."

- "You really disappointed me."

- "He just makes me so mad!"

- "She broke my heart."

Most of us have been conditioned to believe that our emotions are caused by external reality. In a way, this is absolutely true. In the absence of a certain event, we certainly wouldn't emotionally react the same way. But here's the important thing to understand: Yes, a correlation exists between external stimuli and emotional (internal) experience. However, one does not cause the other. External events never cause us to feel how we feel—never.

Imagine standing in the rain and getting soaked. Few people would argue with the notion that the rain is making you wet. It certainly seems this way. After all, if it weren't raining, you wouldn't be getting wet. Obvious, right? Yet this isn't true. There is a correlation between the rain and the fact that you're getting wet, but the rain isn't causing you to get wet; you are. You're getting wet because you made a choice not to use an umbrella, wear a raincoat, or seek shelter. The consequence is caused by you, not by the rain—not by that which is external. Likewise, you may feel annoyed that it's raining. You might complain that the weather is horrible. Is your annoyance caused by the rain? Clearly it isn't, as someone standing next to you in the same deluge might be splashing in puddles and smiling gleefully about it. Neither emotional experience is caused by the rain itself.

Now imagine that someone comes up to you and calls you an asshole. Perhaps you get mad or feel offended. Why? Because that person called you an asshole? What if that same person went up to the Dalai Lama and said the same thing? Would he take offense? Of course not! He would probably chuckle and smile. Why? Because he would likely understand that the comment was merely a reflection of the person who spoke it. We react to external circumstances as we do because of who we are. That's it. If we feel upset or annoyed or hurt, that says something about us, not about our circumstances.

Some plants thrive in the desert sun, while others wither and die. Why? Not because of the nature of sunshine, but because of the differing nature of various plants. It's the same with humans. Everything we experience emotionally says something about us. And when we get upset, our conditioned instinct is typically to attribute this to something external. We think that something external has upset us. This is false. Something within us is the cause. You are responsible for your emotional reactions—just you, not anything or anyone external to you. This is cause for great celebration. Because your emotional reactions are caused by you, you can transform them.

10.

"ALL EMOTIONAL REACTIONS SHARE A SINGLE CAUSE."

This is the concept that changes everything, the truth that flies in the face of conventional thinking and can profoundly and permanently alter your view of yourself, your life, and your ability to create extraordinary relationships. Of everything I've learned in my work as a therapist, nothing has been more influential than the realization that all emotional reactions are caused by the exact same thing.

On the surface, it seems like there's a long list of things that provoke emotional reactions. Maybe you react to your partner crying for no apparent reason, criticizing you, or coming home in a foul mood. Maybe you react to your partner leaving clothes on the floor or forgetting to pay the electricity bill. Maybe you react to someone pulling out in front of you in traffic. Lots of things make you react, right?

Actually, no. There are not a lot of things that make you react. In fact, there's only one. Every time you react, the cause is the same. It isn't another person or an external event; rather, it's your *relationship* to the other person or external event. If your partner starts crying for no apparent reason, criticizes you, or comes home in a foul mood, you react emotionally (and therefore suffer) only if you mind what happens. What causes suffering is your relationship to the event, never the event itself.

When your relationship to an event springs from not giving others or events permission to be what they are, you will react emotionally. That's right, each and every time you react emotionally, the cause is this: you aren't giving permission. That's all there is to it. Let me reiterate to make this point perfectly clear:

You react *only* when you're not giving permission.

And because emotional reactions and suffering are synonymous, the even greater truth is this:

You suffer *only* when you're not giving permission.

This is always true. When you are reacting, you're suffering, and when you're suffering, you're reacting. All the while, the cause is the same. You react and suffer because of one thing and one thing only: You aren't doing something that you could be doing—you aren't giving permission.

The true root of suffering is not giving permission. Of course, there are many people who suffer from severe physical ailments that cannot be fully relieved by giving permission. This approach is not intended to diminish the challenges they face on a daily basis. However, people with physical discomfort can turn their experience into deeper suffering by what they tell themselves about their situation. Negative self-talk can perpetuate suffering. Conversely, realistic and compassionate self-talk, finding ways to befriend pain, looking for its messages, and thanking one's body for doing its best to heal can be much more useful, often helping people move away from suffering and toward an extraordinary relationship with their physical body and its limitations.

Once you understand that your suffering comes mostly from not giving permission, you can embrace your ability to transform it. Since you are the cause, you are also the solution. Permission is always yours to give. In fact, you have an inexhaustible supply of permission to distribute among the people and circumstances of your life. The more you give this extraordinary commodity of yours away, the less you will suffer. Remember:

- All emotional reactions (suffering) come from not giving permission.

- Whenever you feel a way you don't want to be feeling, you aren't giving permission.

- Give permission, and you will transform your suffering.

- Giving permission is the single most important thing you can do to be joyful and build extraordinary relationships.

11.

"YOU WILL CONTINUE TO REACT FOR THE REST OF YOUR LIFE."

Since I'll discuss emotional reactions extensively over the course of this book, let me start by clarifying what emotional reactions are. In and of themselves, they are a normal part of human experience. It's natural and inevitable to react emotionally upon occasion. We humans are prewired to do so and cannot shut off this automatic, autonomic response. When you react emotionally, an event has typically set off chemicals within your brain that lead you toward one of three actions: fighting, fleeing, or freezing.

As to what happens next, you have a choice. You can choose to respond to reactive emotions in healthier ways. For instance, if someone you care for breaks up with you, you might naturally shed a few tears or feel upset. You can even express these emotions in a calm and mature way. That's healthy. What wouldn't be healthy would be responding to your emotional reaction by yelling, screaming, begging this person to stay, or threatening the person. It's how you behave after you react emotionally that matters most. Problems arise not from the emotional reaction itself, but from what customarily happens next—namely fighting, fleeing, or freezing.

Physiologically, you can't prevent yourself from reacting sometimes. That's just life. But what you can prevent is acting out in counterproductive ways when, physiologically, you have reacted to something. That's where giving permission comes in. Between the physiological experience of an emotional reaction and acting out, there's enough time to sidestep reactive behavior and give permission instead. So, when I say that you will continue to react for the rest of your life, I'm referring to the physiological reaction. And luckily, physiological reactions themselves are not problematic. The key is how you behave in response to them.

Some people are highly reactive, while others are much less so. Your current level of emotional reactivity (that is, how often you react physiologically) is a reflection of your current ability to give permission. It's also a reflection of your state of well-being at any given moment. Your ability to give permission can fluctuate depending on a number of variables: the amount of sleep you've gotten, how hungry you are, the time of day or month, and so on. You can get to be really great at giving permission, but you can't be perfect at it. Even if you try to give permission all the time, sometimes you simply won't. That's okay. Giving permission isn't about entirely eliminating your reactions. It's about knowing what to do (and not do) with them when they occur.

Whenever you respond to an emotional reaction not by fighting, fleeing, or freezing but by giving permission, your overall ability at giving permission improves. With consistent practice, you'll find yourself reacting less often and less intensely. You'll start unconsciously giving permission more and more of the time, and many things that used to bother you no longer will, or at least not to the same degree. Eventually, almost all of your emotions will reside within the range in which you feel calm and retain the ability to respond, rather than react. It is possible to live the vast majority of your life within your emotional comfort zone.

Part 2, The Art of Giving Permission, examines what it means to give permission and why this skill is so essential for the cultivation of extraordinary relationships. Indeed, it is so essential that it constitutes the first—and most important—truth about love.

PART 2

THE ART
OF GIVING
PERMISSION

12.

"GIVING PERMISSION ALLEVIATES YOUR OWN SUFFERING."

It would be lovely if things were always exactly the way we want them to be, but it seldom works out that way. That's not life, not reality. But as you now know, reality doesn't makes us suffer; we suffer when we aren't giving permission. Therefore, to suffer less, choose to give permission more. Give permission for your own sake, because you deserve to experience the joyfulness that arises from doing so. Since your joy is your job, this is quite an accomplishment.

What most of us want out of life is fairly simple: to not suffer and to have extraordinary relationships. You can achieve both by mastering the art of giving permission. The key is remembering that whenever you are suffering, whenever you feel upset or angry, impatient or frustrated, irritated or annoyed, you aren't giving permission. In such moments, if you choose to give permission instead, your suffering will diminish. In short, you'll feel better. This is the first goal of giving permission.

Quite often, things probably won't be exactly the way you want them to be. Nonetheless, you deserve not to suffer. This is always true, whether your partner cancels a weekend getaway together at the last moment, you just got a haircut you hate, or the candidate you voted for lost by a landslide. There's never a good reason to make yourself suffer. You can always show yourself the kindness of giving permission instead.

13.
"GIVING PERMISSION DOES NOT REQUIRE APPROVAL."

Most people think giving permission to something implies approval or being okay with it. This belief causes people to balk at giving permission to many things—infidelity or a loved one's addiction, for example. Therefore, it is essential to understand the distinction between giving permission and approval.

You don't have to approve of something in order to give permission. Why? Because giving permission isn't about others; it's about you. Giving permission is the process by which you transform your emotional state from suffering to nonsuffering. Even if you don't approve of something, you can still reduce your own suffering by giving permission. Giving permission is always appropriate because reducing your own suffering is always appropriate. You don't have to approve of something to treat yourself in a compassionate way.

This is probably a bit confusing, so bear with me. Over the course of the next several chapters things will become clearer. For now, just understand that giving permission is an internal process that you can extend toward everything, even toward things you may not approve of. And as you'll learn as you read on, this process can be beneficial not only in helping yourself, but in helping others and in creating extraordinary relationships.

14.
"It's Okay That Things Aren't Okay."

When you look at the world we live in, you probably see many things that seem blatantly *not* okay: domestic violence, child abuse, rape, genocide, world hunger, and global pollution, to name a few. Giving permission is entirely different from saying that something is okay. It's not about abandoning your morality; it's about transforming your emotional experience so you can suffer less and become a skillful agent for change.

Proclaiming that something is not okay does not keep it from existing. As such, you might as well adopt a more useful perspective, a perspective that helps both you and others. After all, it's true, some things *aren't* okay. But this is not a good reason to suffer. You can give permission instead, reminding yourself, *It's okay that things aren't okay.* This changes your *relationship* to what you feel is wrong, thereby decreasing how much you suffer on account of its existence.

If you want to fix a particular problem, you can do so without enduring suffering or jeopardizing your future efforts to be of service. Mahatma Gandhi, Nelson Mandela, Martin Luther King Jr., and Mother Theresa are model examples of people who had serious grievances, things they saw as not okay and wanted to change. However, instead of staying in a state of emotional suffering and acting from a place of anger or indignation, they gave permission and acted from a place of thoughtfulness, compassion, and calm. It is no coincidence that each of these people was successful at creating the changes they desired. Giving permission not only alleviates suffering, it leads to more conscious, mindful, and effective behaviors.

15.
"GIVING PERMISSION IS DIFFERENT THAN ACCEPTANCE."

Imagine yourself on a plane that's crashing. Scary, right? No one would fault you for panicking. Panic would be an understandable emotional reaction caused by not giving permission for the plane to be crashing. Naturally, you don't want to die. So, what to do? Accept this unfortunate situation and embrace your fate?

If you were to accept that the plane is crashing, you might find a measure of peace. You might say a prayer or mentally tell your friends and family good-bye. Sadly, the plane would still crash, and that would be that. Accepting your plight might help a little, but not a lot. What would be better? Giving permission.

If you were to give permission for the plane to be crashing, your panic could subside, and then you could think clearly from a place of calm. You might decide, *I don't accept this situation, and because I don't accept it, I'm going to try to change it.* You might climb out of your seat and make your way to the front of the plane. Peering into the cockpit, you might see that the pilot has had a seizure. Then you could move him to the side, grab the throttle, and halt the plane's descent, saving the day. Bravo!

Giving permission isn't about accepting something the way it is and doing nothing about it. You don't have to tolerate things you don't want or accept things you deem unacceptable. What can you do instead? You can give permission. And by giving permission, you increase your ability to create change. Whether you want to influence a crashing plane or floundering relationship, you can do so best not by accepting or causing an uproar, but by giving permission.

16.

"GIVING PERMISSION MAXIMIZES YOUR ABILITY TO RESPOND."

Think of a matador facing a bull. Standing still, the matador awaits the bull's charge without getting angry or blaming the bull for wanting to gore him. The matador skillfully embraces the dynamic at hand and takes no offense, knowing that none of this is personal. Here, the matador is giving permission for a bull to be a bull.

Giving permission, the matador maintains his calm and maximizes his ability to respond to the bull's aggression without being harmed. Once the bull charges, the matador would quickly regret any decision to charge back or run terrified in the opposite direction. Instead, he calmly holds his cape to the side. When the bull rushes through the cape, the matador remains unscathed. The calmer the matador, the more successful he will be at this.

When faced with any stimulus, you have the ability to emulate the matador. You have the ability to maintain your emotional calm and respond effectively. You can choose to manage your emotional reactions by giving permission. You can't control the external world; you can only control yourself. Whenever you find yourself in a reactive state, you can return to your emotional comfort zone by giving permission. Then you'll be able to respond with greater skill. This is the second goal of giving permission: restoring your ability to respond to your circumstances in the healthiest, most intentional, and most effective ways possible.

17.
"GIVING PERMISSION RESTORES INTENTIONALITY."

While you are within your emotional comfort zone, you can think clearly and act with intention. You can say what you mean to say, do what you mean to do, and behave in ways in keeping with what you want to achieve. Contrast this with what happens when you're in a reactive state.

When the wave of emotion has ascended beyond your comfort zone, you feel a way you don't want to be feeling and are therefore suffering. Perhaps someone asks you to dance at a club, and your hands get clammy and your heart begins to race. As this happens, you lose intentionality. Maybe you notice that the person who asked you to dance looks like your favorite celebrity, increasing the intensity of your emotions. The higher the ascent beyond your comfort zone, the less intentionally you can respond. You might say and do things you don't intend and give less forethought to ramifications. You might stutter, spill your drink, or nervously scurry away. As long as you remain outside your emotional comfort zone, your speech and actions won't be as helpful or intentional.

In an entirely different situation, you might yell at your partner for checking e-mail while you're trying to enjoy a meal together. You might tell someone you love, "I never want to see you again!" You might eat a quart of ice cream or polish off a pint of whiskey. Why? Because you're outside of your emotional comfort zone and reacting, rather than responding from within it.

The times when you're experiencing an emotional reaction are the times when you're most likely to act out. Think of acting out as acting from *outside* your emotional comfort zone. For instance, imagine that you and your partner are at an airport about to board a flight to some exotic destination for a long-awaited holiday. You've worked hard all year and saved your money to afford this adventure, and you have been eagerly anticipating this chance to share quality time together and connect. Suddenly, the gate attendant announces over the loudspeaker that the plane has a mechanical problem and departure will be delayed for an indeterminate amount of time. An hour passes, then another. As your frustration mounts, you complain with ever-increasing fervor about this "rotten situation." Eventually, your partner complains about the fact that you're complaining. Now both of you are probably miserable and bickering. Not only have you failed to solve anything, you've made matters worse—and you definitely aren't enjoying quality time with your partner. Plus, staying reactive has loaded your body full of stress hormones and diminished your ability to think and act effectively, to everyone's detriment.

Although you are understandably displeased with the delay, what if you were to notice your impatience early on and give permission instead? You'd remain calm. Maybe you and your partner would stroll throughout the terminal, exploring the shops. You might decide to buy a great book from the bookstore or a deck of cards to play games together. You might engage fellow passengers in conversation and perhaps meet another couple headed to the same destination. Once you get there, you might even hang out with this couple and commence a lifelong friendship. If you give permission, a bounty of rewarding possibilities can emerge.

When you're outside your emotional comfort zone, you can't benefit yourself or others all that well. You can try, but your suffering will get in the way. The truth is, there's an easier way to go about things. Instead of acting out, you can "act in"—from *inside* your emotional comfort zone. However, this is possible only when you choose to respond to the physiological discomfort of your inevitable emotional reactions by giving permission. Embrace this as not only your ability, but also your responsibility or, as it's sometimes presented, as your response-ability.

18.

"ACTING OUT HARMS RELATIONSHIPS."

Imagine a child who is home painting a picture, something she plans to give to her parents. She expects they'll display it proudly on the refrigerator, like others she painted in the past. In a moment of excitement, she spills some paint on the carpet. Just then, her mom walks in and sees this. How does the mother respond? This depends on whether she's within her emotional comfort zone. If she isn't, her natural physiological reaction (increased heart rate, body tension, elevated cortisol levels, and so on) will probably lead her into fight mode. Perhaps she gets angry and yells at her daughter or calls her clumsy. Why? What's the benefit in having such an unhelpful and ultimately unproductive interaction? What are the costs?

By getting angry and yelling, presumably the mom is trying to teach her daughter that spilling paint is unacceptable, something that must never happen. Unfortunately, because her communication is so wrought with emotion, even if this message is conveyed it comes at a cost. Her connection with her daughter is harmed, maybe a little, maybe a lot. Over time, such interactions can produce long-term negative consequences, such as emotional distance and distrust.

When people act out, they reveal that they aren't being intentional. When we cast the blame for our emotional experience outward, we insinuate that the other person is wrong, bad, or somehow inadequate. This form of rejection then almost always pushes the other person away. Although this probably isn't the goal, it happens nonetheless.

The little girl's mother didn't want to see paint on the rug, so she reacted. We react to things we don't like, things we want to change. And although we are perfectly entitled to want something to be different, acting out isn't the healthiest way to achieve this. Plus, while we're acting out, the paint is still there, soaking into the carpet.

People tend to try to create changes in others in ways that simply don't work or that, at best, work but come at a cost. There's a word for this: "punishment." Punishment is an attempt to diminish the likelihood that a behavior will occur again. When that mother yells at her daughter, she's punishing her. Maybe the daughter won't ever spill paint on the carpet again. Maybe the punishment "works." But, does it work to cultivate a closer, more intimate relationship? Definitely not.

In your relationships, you probably want more trust, harmony, connectedness, and intimacy, even while you seek to foster change. Acting out of your comfort zone won't foster these qualities. So instead of punishing others for not being the way you want them to be, show them that you embrace them as they are. Give permission.

Imagine if the mother had done this, rather than acting out. She could have given permission for her daughter to have spilled the paint, understanding that it was an accident. She could have calmly explained the importance of being careful with paint, and then they might have cleaned up the spill together. In this way, the incident could have become an opportunity to grow closer, rather than farther apart. The daughter would still have learned the lesson, but without the relationship being harmed in the process.

This is precisely what you can accomplish when you choose to manage your emotional reactions. This is no less true with adults than it is with children. If you act out toward your partner, hoping that doing so will curb some particular behavior, then perhaps this form of punishment will be successful. Whether it is or isn't, your relationship will be harmed in the process. Wouldn't it be preferable to achieve the desired result while also *improving* your relationship? Of course! You can avoid the negative consequences of acting out by returning to your emotional comfort zone through choosing to give permission. In doing so, you can inspire change and protect your relationships at the same time.

19.

"JUDGING IS THE OPPOSITE OF GIVING PERMISSION."

All emotional reactions arise from conscious or unconscious judgments: "You're annoying me." "You're being ridiculous." "I can't believe you did that!" "That was so hurtful." "You're too sensitive." Statements like these don't help relationships. They show others that you're being judgmental of them, that you erroneously believe they are causing your suffering. And yet, presumably, you're trying to improve the relationship.

It's impossible to emotionally react to something without some measure of judgment. Even if you're walking through the jungle and a tiger leaps out at you, your emotional reaction belies a judgment, in this case, that it's bad to be attacked by a tiger. Although most people would agree with you, this is still a judgment.

It's normal to react and judge sometimes. That's just the way we humans are. The important thing to understand is how acting out based on judgments can affect your relationships. The bottom line is that no one likes being judged. If you act out from your judgments and emotional reactions instead of giving permission, you give others cause to keep a safe distance from you by behaving in a way that isn't enjoyable to be around.

You can avoid this by letting go of judgments as they arise. You can choose to give permission, which is a way of transforming any judgments you've consciously or unconsciously made about others. Returning to your comfort zone, you can share what precipitated your reaction and then intentionally (and calmly) move toward change together.

20.

"ACTING OUT UNDERMINES FREEDOM."

Everyone wants freedom. Like others, you want the liberty to be who you are, without being condemned for your authentic self. This is all that any of us has ever wanted. Given that we were born with such freedom, where did it go?

In childhood, we learned that when others were happy with us, life was easiest. As others unconsciously blamed their unhappiness on us—through scoldings and reprimands—we began to censor ourselves, not wanting to be subjected to their negative emotional reactions. Indeed, the emotional reactions of others and their subsequent acting out taught us (falsely) that we were not permitted to be ourselves. Simultaneously, we started unconsciously blaming our reactions on others, emulating how others treated us. We learned that acting out of our negative reactions could alter other people's behaviors. Since this appeared to work fairly well, most of us kept up with this approach, even if it didn't feel good.

As adults, many of us still operate as we did in childhood. We let how others act out dictate how we behave, and we act out toward others in an attempt to alter how they are in relationship to us. Although this harms more than helps, we've been trained to live this way. To achieve extraordinary relationships—not just with other people, but with yourself and your life—commit to transforming this unhelpful conditioning. Replace old habits with a healthier approach. Embrace your own freedom and encourage the freedom of others. Give permission for others to be as they are, whether or not you like how they are. When you do this, you will not only ease your suffering, you'll extend to others the rare and extraordinary gift of complete embrace and freedom.

21.

"PEOPLE WILL FIGHT LIKE HELL FOR FREEDOM, AND RIGHTFULLY SO."

Whenever we react to others, presumably there's something about them that we don't like. Maybe it's a comment they made or some action we've deemed irritating. If we act out from our emotional reaction, perhaps telling them that they shouldn't have said or done something, this comes across as an attempt to limit their freedom. Whenever people feel their freedom is threatened, they're likely to react in turn. They may retaliate or try to find a way to escape the relationship. People will fight like hell for their freedom, and rightfully so.

I remember one married couple, both on their third marriage, who fought almost constantly, mainly because they seemed to want two different things. The wife was a staunchly independent workaholic who spent her days running her own business and enjoyed staying up late each night spending time alone. She felt claustrophobic in her new home, her husband's small apartment in the city, and consistently complained of feeling trapped and wanting more space. The husband, who was retired, craved more of his wife's time, attention, and affection. The more he struggled to get these things, the more aggressive she was toward him, to the point where she was strongly considering divorce.

What was going on? The wife was fighting like hell for her freedom to live her life as she pleased without feeling obligated to satisfy the emotional demands of her husband. In fact, the more he lobbied for what he wanted, the more she perceived him as weak and needy. She increasingly lost respect for him and wanted to be around him even less. All the while, she wasn't getting what she wanted (space and freedom) and he wasn't getting what he wanted (time and affection). Now they were drifting apart, growing increasingly emotionally distant. How to reverse this?

The remedy was for the husband to give permission for his wife to want what she wanted: to move back to her house in the country and live and work from there, without him. Did this signify the end of their marriage? Not in the least. Actually, when he gave his wife this permission, he found that she started choosing to spend more time together. As a result, they started going out more and enjoying each other as they had when they first met. Why? Because they were both getting what they wanted. The wife got her space and independence; the husband got the time and affection he had so desired. This didn't take negotiation or even a lot of therapy. It just took opening an avenue of freedom through giving permission.

Of course, giving freedom doesn't guarantee that a couple will stay together and live happily ever after. The husband might have given his wife permission to spend time away from him only to find that she decided she was happier alone. If so, they would have divorced—and that would have been for the best. The only guarantee is that a refusal to give freedom and permission leads to strife and estrangement. Had they not chosen to honor freedom, this couple could have gone on being resentful and miserable with one another for a long, long time. Why bother? It's better to support freedom completely—through giving permission—and see what happens.

22.

"WHAT DOES THE IDEAL RELATIONSHIP LOOK LIKE?"

How can you tell when a relationship is successful? What distinguishes your favorite relationships from others? What is it about your relationship with, for instance, your very best friend that makes it what it is?

The answer is simple: how comfortable you feel when you're around this person. And what creates this sense of comfort? The fact that you know this person likes you just the way you are. We feel closest to those who judge us the least, who embrace us with little or no complaint and criticism. Around such people, we know we can be fully ourselves. We can share anything and don't have to walk on eggshells so as not to offend them. This feels good. In fact, it feels extraordinary.

Everyone wants to feel that they are okay. When others know that you embrace them completely, when they know that you won't judge them for what they think, feel, say, or do—even things you may not like—it creates an unwavering sense of interconnectedness and intimacy. People feel closest to those who like them for who they are, plain and simple.

Understanding that this is what you yourself want, you can choose to provide this for others—to be a person who embraces and appreciates others exactly as they are. Giving permission in this way is the very foundation of extraordinary relationships.

23.

"THE CHOICE TO BE IN A RELATIONSHIP IS THE CHOICE TO EMBRACE 100 PERCENT."

If you're going to have a relationship with someone, why not aim to make it extraordinary? When you see the choice to be in a relationship as the choice to embrace someone 100 percent, as difficult as this may sometimes be, you take a stand. You *aspire* to an extraordinary relationship rather than settling for less. It's like saying, "I am going to be this for you because I can. There aren't many people in the world who treat you in this extraordinary way, so let me extend this superior kindness to you."

Indeed, the kindness that comes from giving permission may be the highest form of kindness you can show someone. Why not aspire to fully embrace others as they are, 100 percent? If you later discover that you're unwilling to embrace 100 percent, that you simply want something different, you can choose 0 percent. You can opt out of your own suffering and free others from the pain of relating to someone who wants them to be different. We all perpetually retain the right to leave, and if we are unwilling to embrace another fully, leaving would be an act of kindness. Everyone deserves to be in a relationship with someone who embraces them fully: 100 percent, not 5 percent, not 50 percent, and not even 90 percent or 95 percent. In extraordinary relationships, you have two choices: 100 percent or 0 percent. Of course, you can't choose 0 percent with some people, such as your parents, your children, or yourself. As such, in those cases 100 percent is your only option!

Right now you might be thinking, *What if I want to have a relationship with someone I don't accept 100 percent? What if I want my partner to change a few things about himself?* Actually, that isn't a problem. As discussed earlier, giving permission is different than acceptance. In fact, the process of giving permission is very much about change: changing yourself, changing others, and changing your relationships. Aspiring to embrace 100 percent just happens to be the prerequisite for this.

Fighting for change and insisting that others be different simply doesn't work. The truth is, you can inspire change more effectively by giving permission than by withholding it. If you want a specific change, why not give embracing a try? Let others know that you embrace them as they are, that they don't need to make the desired change for you, that they are okay just the way they are. Instead of trying to change them, give permission. Then, while giving permission, you can tell them how a particular detail about them tends to affect you.

Let's look at an example: Imagine that every time your partner wears a specific red shirt you break into hives. You don't know why this happens, but it does. Instead of telling him how much you hate that shirt or demanding that he stop wearing it, you can inform him of this phenomenon: "I've noticed that every time you wear that shirt I break into hives. I'm not sure why this happens, but I just thought I'd tell you." That's good information for your partner. In fact, chances are he'll immediately stop wearing it, at least around you, completely on his own. You've managed to change the relationship without insisting that your partner change. And on the off chance that he wears that shirt regardless, this would tell you something about him. Maybe it would tell you that leaving this relationship would be the path to take.

When you view your choice to be in a relationship as the choice to embrace 100 percent, you respect others' right to be who they are, exactly as they are, in that moment. Fighting how they are changes nothing, so you might as well give permission. Allow others to be how they are in the moment—not indefinitely, not forever, just in that moment. By doing so, you can reduce suffering in the relationship. Then you can both learn and grow together. This is the power of giving permission.

24.
"ACTING IN IS THE ANSWER."

Clearly, acting out can be extremely detrimental to you, to others, and to your relationships. When you act from outside your emotional comfort zone, it's unlikely that any good will come from it. Whatever you do or say will be unintentional and not as helpful as a response that comes from a state of emotional calm. If you act from a place of emotional reaction, the other person will probably do the same, perpetuating all-too-familiar patterns of conflict. Sabrina fittingly dubbed this cycle the "loop of doom." In this vicious cycle, the reactions of each person trigger stronger reactions in the other—onward and upward—until the conflict escalates to a breaking point. The more such cycles recur, the more they erode harmony in the relationship. You can avoid this by choosing to "act in."

After experiencing emotional reactions, you have a choice between acting out and acting in. To avoid the loop of doom and act in, give permission. Doing so transforms your emotional reactions, restores calm, and enables intentional responses. Having restored your calm, you will now be able to respond with intention; you'll be able to act in rather than out. Doing so, you focus your attention on creating extraordinary relationships without wasting your (or your partner's) time and energy in damaging conflicts. As you master the art of giving permission, you'll find that not only are you capable of getting along amazingly well with anyone, but that you can influence change in profound and loving ways.

25.
AN EXAMPLE OF
PERMISSION IN ACTION

Matthew, a successful lawyer, came to me because he was frustrated with his relationship with his younger brother. He was furious at his sibling, who he described as a worthless junkie. Indeed, his brother wasn't in good shape. He had moved to a distant city, where he was homeless, using drugs, and dealing drugs to support his habit. Matthew's mother was perpetually distraught about this and often complained to Matthew about it. Matthew wanted to help, but his many attempts to get his brother to reform had failed. Matthew was at his wits' end, clueless as to how to help his mother or his brother. Actually, Matthew was fairly certain that his brother was a lost cause, but it still tortured him to see his mother suffer so intensely. He wanted desperately to help.

I wasn't surprised that Matthew's previous attempts to intervene had failed. Although his efforts were well-intentioned, they were characterized by compassionately trying to encourage his brother to change. For example, he might say, "Come on, man. What are you doing? Don't you see how you are destroying Mom—and yourself, for that matter? You're too good for this. You don't have to live this way. Seriously, let me help you. Let's get you clean." This hadn't worked, and it never would.

I suggested to Matthew that there was an alternative approach: giving permission. This philosophy immediately appealed to him, and after about a month of therapy, Matthew booked a flight to the city where his brother lived. Once there, he walked the neighborhoods his brother frequented, asked around, and eventually found him on a street corner. Now face-to-face, Matthew told his brother that he simply wanted to see him "just to say hi and connect." He didn't say anything about wanting his brother to quit using drugs.

Rather, he told his brother that he loved him just the way he was, that he didn't have to change, and that he was perfectly fine as he was, in essence giving his brother permission to be homeless, addicted to drugs, and struggling. He told him, "You're my brother and I love you. That's it." They spent a few days together, then Matthew went back home. The next week, Matthew's mother called and said, "I wanted you to know that I just got off the phone with your brother. He's checked himself into rehab."

This is exactly how giving permission works to create change. When you give others permission to be who and how they are, you show them that they are okay, just as they are. Showing others love in this extraordinary way is highly nourishing. As a result, their confidence and belief in themselves grow. Instead of judging themselves as flawed or inadequate (as others have probably done), they now begin to embrace themselves as you have embraced them, emulating the permission you have given. They start to experience themselves as okay, just as they are. From this self-embrace comes a profound sense of power. Feeling stronger, they become more capable of accomplishing whatever it is they truly want. Surprisingly often, this is what you've been wanting for them as well. Giving permission is a potent tool for influencing change, and although it may seem counterintuitive, it works. So in part 3 of the book, we'll take a closer look at how to give permission.

PART 3

HOW TO GIVE
PERMISSION

26.
"GIVING PERMISSION IS AN ART."

Becoming masterful at giving permission will take time and patience. As with any art, your abilities will grow with practice. However, practice alone is not enough. Artists are very familiar with this. You can paint dozens of canvases and still not significantly evolve as an artist because without learning new techniques, you're less likely to produce different results.

Giving permission is similar. It takes practice, but it takes technique too, and those techniques are what this section offers. With these techniques and a commitment to practice them, you can indeed become masterful at this new art. Giving permission is an art that's accomplished in five key steps, which I'll explain fully in this part of the book:

1. Recognizing that you're outside your emotional comfort zone

2. Pausing to consider your options

3. Breathing to restore calm and present-moment awareness

4. Understanding that giving permission is always both beneficial and justified

5. Actually giving permission

Giving permission may be difficult at first. It probably won't feel natural. Still, just keep at it and notice the results you achieve along the way. When you see how well giving permission works, you'll be even more motivated to practice, and the more you practice, the easier giving permission will become.

Even an action as simple as throwing a ball is composed of several steps. You grasp the ball in your hand, move your arm backward, pivot at the waist, heave your arm forward, then release the ball toward your target. When you throw a ball, do you consider each of these steps? Probably not. You simply throw the ball in a single fluid motion. With practice, giving permission will be the same way. You'll be able to do it in a single fluid motion, with little or no thought at all.

Just the other day, a client I hadn't seen in a while dropped by for a visit. She told me, "It's funny. I used to make an effort to give permission, but now it just happens without my trying or thinking about it. I'm basically giving permission all the time now. Who knew life could feel so wonderful!" This is possible for you too, if you commit to practicing this art regularly.

27.

"YOU ARE NEARLY AN EXPERT AT GIVING PERMISSION."

I have great news! Giving permission hinges upon your ability to do something you already know how to do extremely well. Actually, you're nearly an expert at it. For virtually all of your life, you have been unconsciously giving permission almost incessantly. This very moment, you are giving permission. You're giving permission for these words in print to look the way they do, permission for your clothes to feel as they do against your skin, permission for the air to contact your face the way it is right now. On and on, you are giving permission, almost constantly, and feeling comfortable all the while.

The only exceptions, the only instances when the ability to give permission falters, are those moments when we experience emotional reactions that move us outside our comfort zone. These comparatively rare instances provide opportunities to make a choice to *consciously* do something that you usually do unconsciously: give permission. When you learn specific steps for giving permission, your ability to do so, both consciously and unconsciously, will steadily improve.

Meanwhile, take solace in knowing that cultivating extraordinary relationships by means of giving permission involves doing something you already know how to do exceptionally well. You're just going to get even better at it.

28.
STEP 1: RECOGNIZING

It's difficult to change something you're unaware of. Since the goal is to transform unhelpful reactions when they arise, the first step in the process of giving permission is recognizing when you're outside of your emotional comfort zone.

Once you recognize that you're in a reactive state, simply note to yourself, *Oh, I'm not giving permission right now! If I give permission, I'll feel better and respond in a healthier way.* This begins the process of replacing old patterns of interacting with something new. Only when you recognize that you aren't giving permission can you choose to give permission instead.

Indeed, every time you're in a reactive state, your mind is probably lost in thoughts about some personal grievance—how something about yourself or your circumstances or another person isn't the way you want it to be. Your instinct may be to fixate on what you think has provoked your emotional reaction. Instead of traveling down that familiar road of upset or irritation, admit what's really going on: You're not giving permission.

Over the next couple of days, check in with your emotions often. Envision the shifting intensity of your emotions at certain moments and ask yourself, *Am I inside my comfort zone or outside it? If inside, where exactly? If outside, by how much?* Get to know your emotional states so you can better recognize when you aren't giving permission. Then, whenever you catch yourself, you'll be able to begin transforming your emotional state by moving to step 2: pausing.

29.
STEP 2: PAUSING

Imagine hiking along a mountain trail and coming to a place where the path forks. What would you do? You'd probably pause and consider which path to take. You might look for a sign that points toward your desired destination. If no sign exists, you'd make an educated guess. If you wish to hike into a canyon, you might pick the fork that heads downward; if climbing a peak, might pick the path that climbs most steeply. Either way, you'd probably pause before deciding. You wouldn't barrel down one trail or the other without a moment's hesitation.

Whenever we experience an emotional reaction, we arrive at a fork in our path. Unfortunately, most people don't recognize this and barrel along without hesitation, oblivious to the fact that they're taking a turn for the worse. When the trail inevitably leads to thorny brambles or disappears entirely, people become perplexed, wondering how they got there. The answer is simple: they missed the other path, the path of giving permission.

Step 1 acknowledges the importance of recognition. Giving permission begins with recognizing that you've come to a fork in the trail. What can alert you that this has happened? Your emotional reaction and the fact that you're feeling a way you don't want to be feeling. Chances are your level of dopamine, the neurotransmitter that creates a higher possibility for positive moods, has dropped, and your level of cortisol, a stress hormone, is rising. You can't control this cascading autonomic response, which is wired into your emotions, but you can control what comes next by pausing. This is step 2.

When you pause, you can better consider your options. You aren't obligated to race down a path that will ultimately lead you into peril or get you lost. When you're in a reactive state, you aren't obligated to act right away. You can give yourself a moment to gather your thoughts and weigh the choices available to you. If you don't know what to say to help your situation, say nothing until you do. This is the immense benefit of pausing: it keeps you from ending up where you know you don't want or intend to go.

Pausing while recognizing yourself in a reactive state safeguards you and your relationships from injury. This is a lot like following the "do no harm" principle found in the Hippocratic oath, the oath traditionally sworn by physicians. Although your goal may be to create healing, first and foremost, it is important to do no harm. Since you know that acting out is harmful, pause. If you don't know how to improve your current situation, that's okay. Give yourself a moment. Understand that now is not the time to do or say anything. Focus your energies instead on transforming your emotion by completing the remaining steps of giving permission. Only when this is accomplished will you be capable of creating change in a healthy and healing way.

30.
STEP 3: BREATHING

Breathing is easier than giving permission, especially when you're experiencing an emotional reaction. While you may not always feel capable of giving permission at these times, you're certainly capable of breathing. And if after step 2, pausing, you take a moment to breathe, your emotion will descend toward your comfort zone, where it's easier to think clearly. As your emotion calms in this way, even if only a little, your ability to choose which path to take will be enhanced.

Step 3, breathing, actually involves more than simply breathing. Your reactions are more than oxygen deprivation, so oxygen alone will not suffice to transform them. The combination of oxygen and mindfulness can, however, do the trick.

Thich Nhat Hanh, a Vietnamese Buddhist monk who has written numerous books on mindfulness, recommends one traditional mantra that I have found so effective at restoring calm that I utilize it several times daily—anytime I notice myself approaching the boundary of my emotional comfort zone. It goes like this: While inhaling slowly, say in your mind, *Breathing in, I know that I am breathing in...* Extend this statement over the entire duration of your inhalation, and let it be a true statement. *Know* that you are breathing in as you silently say these words to yourself, feeling the breath as it enters your body through your nose, moves into your chest and lungs, and fills every cell of your being.

Then do the same as you slowly exhale, saying in your mind, *Breathing out, I know that I am breathing out...* Again, let this be a true statement. Fully know that you are breathing out, bringing your complete mindful awareness to experiencing this. If this exercise doesn't help you return to your emotional comfort zone in a single cycle, that's okay. Just repeat the process until it does. With practice, you'll find that you can usually return to a calm state in just one breath. Then it will be easier for you to give permission.

The real benefit of this exercise comes from present-moment awareness. When you're in an emotionally reactive state, your mind and body are actually disconnected. Your body is doing its thing in the present moment, just being and breathing, but your mind is off in the la-la land of the past or future. If you're reacting, then you're probably mentally in the past. Even if it's only the very recent past, it's still the past. Alternatively, you could be suffering from thoughts about the future: fears or worries about things that haven't occurred yet and may never occur. Whether you're distracted by the past or the future, you aren't in the present. When you take the time to breathe and know that you are breathing, you bring the mind back into connection with the body, the breath, and this present moment. As your mind reconnects with the present moment, you'll return to your emotional comfort zone and feel calm again. Therefore, you pause not only to breathe, but to bring awareness to your breathing.

Practice this often: "Breathing in, I know that I am breathing in… Breathing out, I know that I am breathing out…" Commit these exact words to memory and start using them. Consider writing this mantra on a small note card so you don't forget it. At least two or three times each day, pause for a moment to breathe and know that you are breathing. Then notice the difference this makes in your emotional experience. Those few moments will be profoundly beneficial.

To recap, you've learned the first three steps of giving permission: You *recognize* that you're in a reactive state. You *pause*. And then you *breathe*. Engaging in these first three steps will restore your intentionality, enhancing your ability to consciously give permission.

31.
STEP 4: UNDERSTANDING

Recognition, pausing, and breathing help us manage emotional reactions. This creates the opportunity to choose to give permission. Still, you might wonder if it makes sense to give permission.

Indeed, if you don't like something or don't approve of it, you might find it difficult to give permission. Even if you try, you might not really mean it. While that's totally normal, giving permission works only when it's genuine. That's why the fourth step of giving permission is understanding.

There are two things to understand: The first is how giving permission alleviates your suffering and maximizes your ability to interact in constructive ways, benefiting both you and your relationships. The second thing to understand, which is usually harder, is that giving permission is not only beneficial, but justified. Yes, giving permission is always justified. The more you understand this, the easier (and more sincere) giving permission will be.

Why is it genuinely okay for your partner to chew with her mouth open or watch TV until 2 a.m. most nights? Why is it genuinely okay for your boss to be condescending or for drivers to tailgate you? Why is it okay for the weather to be what it is or for you to look the way you do right now? Why is everything okay, just the way it is? The next two chapters answer these questions.

32.

"EVERYONE DESERVES TO BE GIVEN PERMISSION."

What if everything you think, feel, say, or do is simply a perfect reflection of who you are at any moment? What if you are always merely a product of your vast history of experiences plus a little genetics? Did you choose your genetics? Did you choose your experiences—those events that have shaped and molded you since your birth, making you who you are today? Did you choose your DNA? Did anyone else choose theirs?

Everything happens for a reason, and a good reason at that. You don't need to know the reasons why people think, feel, say, or do what they do. It is enough to know that there are reasons, whatever they may be. Perhaps the man who snoops into his partner's e-mail distrusts because his last two partners cheated on him. Perhaps the cashier who is rude to you just found out her mother has terminal cancer. Perhaps the person who treats you with disdain secretly feels inferior. The reasons are always there.

You are the way you are not by choice, but because of genetics mixed with an intricate synthesis of historical influences and experiences that have shaped you into the individual you are today. You think what you think, feel what you feel, say what you say, and do what you do because, well, that's who you are. Is that a little too obvious to mention? Perhaps. However, as easy as this is to understand about ourselves, we often seem to forget that this is equally true of others.

When you understand and embrace the reality that everything others think, feel, say, or do reveals something about them (and nothing at all about you), then you'll understand that there's no reason to take any of this personally. If your partner slams a door in your face or storms out of the room in a huff, that's information about who and how he is. If someone in traffic gives you the finger, that's information about her. If someone calls you a loser, that's information about him. You can leave it at that. Simply sit back and observe others revealing themselves to you. There is absolutely no need to make any of it into something about you. People are who they are, end of story.

Consider the type of person you are. What qualities most define your personality? What are some of your shortcomings or so-called flaws? Ask yourself how you became this way. Why do you think what you think, feel what you feel, say what you say, and do what you do? Did you choose to be this way? Did others choose to be how they are? Of course not. So you might as well give permission for people, yourself included, to be exactly as they are because, in truth, we all have less say in who we are than it appears. We can shape who we are becoming, but not how we have become up until now.

When you understand that everything others think, feel, say, and do is just information about how they have been shaped by their experiences and genetics, none of which they themselves have chosen, giving permission will be a genuine act on your part. You can understand that no one is actually at fault for how they are. In fact, with a little wisdom, you can even come to understand that, at all times, everyone is, quite honestly, doing the best they can. Although this may be a foreign concept, it's an important one to grasp in order to understand why giving permission is always justified.

Obviously, you rarely get upset at people when you perceive they are doing their best. Why? Because you understand that their effort is what matters most. If others are doing their best, that's all you can ask. But what if everyone, at all times, is actually doing their best? What would the implications be? Would there ever be a legitimate reason to get upset at someone?

Think of a child who throws a tantrum because she doesn't want to leave the zoo. Does she choose this behavior intentionally? Sure, she might gain something by acting out in this way, but is her behavior a conscious choice? If she were capable of saying, "Mother, Father, excuse me, but I was wondering if we might be able to stay a bit longer. I was really hoping to take another gander at the Bengal tiger. That was a most interesting creature," wouldn't she have chosen that form of communication instead? When a baby giggles or cries, that's automatic; it's the best way she knows how to communicate her joy or distress. She's doing the best she can with the tools she has.

No one deliberately chooses to react in immature or ungraceful ways. When upset, some people may punch their fist into a wall, some may run away, some may break down and cry. Why? Because this is the best they can do in the moment. I guarantee that the person who punches a wall doesn't want to punch the wall, the person who runs away doesn't want to run away, and the person who breaks down and cries doesn't want to break down and cry. I guarantee that no one would choose these actions if they had an actual choice in the matter. If they could maintain their calm and handle the situation more gracefully and maturely, they would do so. All of us would.

Everyone is always doing the best they can with the tools they've been given. These tools, which are expressed through thoughts, feelings, speech, and actions, are a by-product of past experiences and innate disposition, none of which are chosen. We are how we are. Others are how they are.

What does this mean for us now? Are we fated to act unconsciously in ways that are beyond our control at any given time? Do we not have free will? Do we not have choice? This is where it gets a bit trickier. In a way, we don't have a choice, and in a way, we do.

Everyone's ability (or inability) to make intentional choices is itself a reflection of their individual upbringing and genetics. Some people live highly intentionally, while others do not. Why? Not because their wants are different, but because their abilities are. Our personal developmental histories have shaped everything about us, including our ability to consciously choose new behaviors. As we exercise our ability to make choices in the present moment, we become more capable of living intentionally in the future. We'll be able to make choices that were previously unavailable to us. We'll still be doing our best, but our best will look and feel different.

The popular notion about people having vast, untapped potential is, in my opinion, more than a bit flawed. This notion suggests that everyone has an amount of potential that has yet to be realized. It's like each of us has a gas tank that can be filled more than it currently is. Maybe we've only realized half of our potential. If so, our tank is filled halfway and can be filled that much again. Presumably, this perspective can inspire us toward greatness, reminding us that we can become better than we are right now. I don't have a problem with the idea that we can achieve more than we have already; I know that we can. However, I think about it differently. I think of each person's tank as being filled to the brim at all times, that in every moment each of us has realized our full potential—our full potential up until now, that is. What changes is not how much gas there is in the tank, but the *size* of the tank.

Your potential changes with each and every new thing you experience. This may seem like a subtle distinction, but it is an important one, and key to embracing the truth that everyone is always doing the best they can. If you see the tank as something that has yet to be filled, then you may perceive within yourself and others a certain degree of deficiency or inadequacy. If, instead, you see the tank as always filled to the brim and understand that as the tank itself grows, it remains filled at all times, then you will never imagine that others could or should be any way other than who and how they are in each moment.

When you understand that people's rough edges (and your own) are merely a reflection of their current abilities, then giving permission makes sense. Rather than condemning others (or yourself) for not being more skillful, you can create a new context that won't harm the relationship and may actually augment these abilities.

The next time you find yourself upset or irritated at others, practice the first four steps of giving permission: recognize, pause, breathe, and understand that others are being (or have been) the best and only version of themselves they can be. As you embrace this knowledge, you'll find that you're now able to give permission—and give it sincerely.

33.
THE ABCs PALETTE OF UNDERSTANDING

Initially, as you begin this worthwhile and powerful process of giving permission, you'll sometimes struggle to understand why giving permission to others (and yourself) is merited. After all, this is a completely new way to think about things—a way that probably runs counter to much of what you've been taught up until now. Achieving such a tremendous paradigm shift isn't always easy, no matter how beneficial doing so may be. Seeing this, Sabrina developed this tool that might help you: the ABCs palette of understanding. You can use this palette to help you paint a new understanding for yourself during the times when giving permission seems difficult or confusing.

Along the way, remember that giving permission is always warranted because it benefits any circumstance. It makes sense to do something that both alleviates your suffering and increases your ability to nurture change. When you realize you deserve to not suffer, that alone justifies giving permission. Still, you might find yourself evaluating whether or not it is appropriate to give permission to certain things or whether others deserve to be given permission. Allow yourself to stop evaluating. Everyone—yes, everyone, at all times, regardless of what they have done or said or felt—deserves to be given permission. The ABCs palette of understanding can help you conduct this artistic endeavor, reminding you to see yourself and others with compassion, patience, and kindness. Use it and you will find yourself able to give permission in a genuine way.

As with any artistic pursuit, it is wise to have some of the essentials before you begin your creative process, in this case, creating extraordinary relationships through giving permission. Starting out, keep in mind that, at any given moment, we each possess certain relational skills, determined by our genetics and conditioning. In a way, these skills constitute our artist's supply kit, or what is available for us to work with in each situation that arises. As you gain more supplies, the size of your kit grows and giving permission authentically comes with greater ease.

You can think of the ABCs as individual tubes of paint to work with as you strive to create understanding. Together, they can indeed be used like a palette of paints. You can blend and mix these colors of understanding until what shows up on the canvas of your relationships is your own rendition of giving permission to yourself, others, and the myriad of situations that life presents you. In other words, this is not a stepwise process (A then B then C), but an experiment in instinctually mixing colors that share the dimensional qualities of the same thing: the loving-kindness of true understanding.

A: Abilities. Actions are a reflection of people's abilities in the moment and are based on the relationship skills and knowledge they bring with them up to this point. For example, say your husband is setting up his fantasy football team during what used to be your morning coffee and connection time. You might think, *The nerve!* Or, thinking of his abilities, you could remind yourself with equanimity, *This is a reflection of his ability to engage with me at the moment. He's simply occupying a different part of his brain right now.*

B: Best effort. The truth is, everyone is always doing their best. This is probably the most useful of all the ABCs, which are in some ways shades of this one understanding. Remembering this vital point during all interactions, with anything or anyone, will help you more easily give permission. For example, say your partner has just arrived home after being away on business all week. She decides to take a conference call the same night she arrives, delaying your plans to go out for dinner. You might think, *I haven't seen her for a week and she still wants to work rather than be with me!* Or you could remind yourself, after breathing and pausing, *She is doing the best she* *can to create a work-life balance. I'm glad that she is so motivated to excel professionally.*

C: Choicelessness. In any given moment, we have no other choice in our thinking, feeling, or behavior. If we did, in difficult moments we would surely select a healthier response. For example, say your girlfriend seems withdrawn when you tell her you are going to go have a beer with your buddy. You're taken aback by her cold shoulder. You might think, *Why does she have to be so needy?* Or you could reflect, *This is her way of communicating to me that she wants us to spend time together. She just doesn't have access to other choices in thinking, feeling, and behaving right now.*

D: Disposition. We are all shaped by our particular genetic disposition. For example, say your boyfriend loses his car keys for the hundredth time. You might think, *What a nincompoop!* Or, rather than judging him, you might consider that this is a manifestation of his biological makeup: *It must be challenging to be so forgetful. Maybe I can help him look for his keys.*

E: Experiences. We are all the sum total of our life experiences up to now. For example, say your partner scoffs when you tell him you've decided to quit work and go back to school to study visual arts. You might think, *He never supports anything I do!* Or you could consider how his life experiences have shaped his opinion: *He was raised to believe that happiness comes from financial security and a steady job that pays well. I can see why he would not understand my decision.*

F: Freedom. Everyone has the freedom, within legal limits, to live a life of their own choosing. For example, say you ask your girlfriend for a ride to the airport and she says she's too busy. You might think, *She never does anything for me! I've driven her to the airport plenty of times.* Or you could remember that, like everyone, she has a right to do as she pleases: *She's attending to other responsibilities in her life right now, and that's okay. I can take a cab.*

The more adept you become at using the colors on this palette, the easier it will be for you to wholeheartedly give permission. The more you paint understanding into life's situations, both simple and complex, the more giving permission becomes second nature, until you find that it has become part of the way you live. If one color is not working, move to another. Blend, dabble, and dip your paintbrush into whichever ones best help you understand the situation or person involved. Sometimes it may take four colors, other times one or two, and still other times, you might have to work with mixing all six to achieve understanding. Regardless of the shades you choose, this will set in motion your ability to give permission and give it sincerely. Then you can help to influence change for the benefit of all, in even the most complicated of situations. What emerges from this process will be something glorious to behold: an extraordinary relationship.

34.
STEP 5: GIVING PERMISSION

The final step in giving permission is, well, giving permission. After you have recognized yourself in a reactive state, paused, taken a mindful breath, and understood why it makes sense to give permission, then you can make a conscious choice to give permission.

In such moments, it might help to ask yourself, *What is the permission I am not giving?* It's always there somewhere. Maybe you're not giving permission to your partner to have said what she said, to have done what she did, to have thought what she thought, or to have felt what she felt. Maybe you're not giving permission for traffic to be snarled or for a popular restaurant to have lost your reservation. Maybe you're not giving yourself permission to be imperfect somehow.

In moments of emotional discomfort, if you look hard enough for where you aren't giving permission, you can always find it. Then you can choose to give the person or situation permission to be what it is, because the alternative, not giving permission, helps no one and solves nothing.

What does giving permission sound like? Maybe something like *This is okay. I give permission to everything to be what it is in the moment, for my benefit and everyone else's.* This is just one example. In time, you'll find your own words for this.

Withholding permission never changes the past and only harms the present and future. It increases your suffering and interferes with your ability to create the changes you desire. Giving permission bolsters your ability to create change. Because of this, the more you detest something, the greater incentive you have to give permission. Take a moment to fathom how ironic this is!

35.

REFLECTION POINT: GIVING PERMISSION

Eventually, giving permission will become instinctual. In the meantime, whenever you notice yourself outside your emotional comfort zone, make a conscious choice to give permission by following the five-step process we've outlined:

1. **Recognize** when your emotion has risen out of your comfort zone. Remember, whenever you feel a way you don't want to be feeling, you're outside your comfort zone.

2. **Pause** when you notice that you're in a reactive state. You don't have to say or do anything right away. Give yourself an opportunity to "do no harm."

3. **Breathe** with mindfulness to reconnect with your experience in the present moment. This will help you start thinking more clearly, making it easier to achieve the next step.

4. **Understand** that it always makes sense to give permission, for two reasons. First, it helps you suffer less and respond better. Second, everyone deserves to be given permission (recall the ABCs palette of understanding).

5. **Give permission** for yourself, others, and your circumstances to be as they are. This will restore your calm, allowing you to pursue change in intentional and effective ways.

You are well on the way to creating extraordinary relationships and might be starting to wonder, *What comes next?* After you've managed your emotional reactions and are better able to respond with intention, what responses will be most helpful in creating the changes you desire? This is where the wisdom of taking responsibility comes in.

36.
THE WISDOM OF TAKING RESPONSIBILITY

By this point you know that emotional reactions occur because you aren't giving permission. The next time this happens, you'll know what to do. Having recognized this, you'll know that the next steps are to pause, breathe, understand why it makes sense to give permission, and then give it.

Giving permission is profound. It will enable you to consciously strive toward specific goals by responding in constructive ways—something that's possible only while you're giving permission, and something that's impossible while you aren't. Interestingly, when you're giving permission, taking responsibility is much easier, and it is the wisdom of taking responsibility that cultivates change.

If you think of a relationship as being like a sailboat, giving permission would be the sails, and taking responsibility would be the rudder and helm. They work together to successfully transport you. Giving permission propels; taking responsibility steers. Without the momentum of giving permission, there would be no point in turning the rudder, and taking the helm would be pointless. With wind in your sails but no rudder or helm, you'd be very unlikely to reach your preferred destination. The journey might be enjoyable, but it won't be the journey you wished to take. You can, however, navigate your relationships (and yourself) toward any destination you choose by first giving permission, and then taking responsibility.

37.
"YOU CAN ALWAYS INFLUENCE CHANGE."

As discussed, giving permission isn't about tolerating suffering; it's about transforming it. It's compassionate to desire improvements in your life, yourself, your relationships, and even others. In fact, this is a profoundly healthy ambition. The key is to go about fostering change in a way that is effective.

If you try to change others, your efforts may be interpreted as controlling. If people think you're trying to control them, they may resent you, fight you, or simply avoid you. If you try to control others and fail, you may come to resent them for not changing. This actually happens quite often, as in the case of John and Bill, who have been partners for seven years and exhibit a fairly common pattern of communicating in their relationship. John tries to control Bill's drinking by complaining and is unsuccessful, and then he becomes increasingly angry at Bill for not changing. John's frustration increases, leading to increased efforts to get Bill to drink less, with John growing progressively more resentful along the way. Meanwhile, Bill, whose freedom and fallibility are being rejected, feels judged and responds with increasing intensity and force. Conflict escalates, and the emotional distance in the relationship grows for both of the men. Bill might even begin to drink more—the exact opposite of what John intended.

The bottom line? Controlling never works. Influence, on the other hand, always works. Influence always works because it doesn't always work. Huh? Let me explain.

The truth is, influence always works because when you choose to influence rather than control, you embrace an understanding that others or circumstances may or may not change as a result of your efforts. This approach acknowledges that you can do only so much. Influence works not because it allows you to dictate the behaviors of others (control), but because it gives others permission to succeed in measure with their abilities. When you aim for influence, you're less likely to become resentful of others or fault them (or yourself) for things not turning out the way you may have hoped—and others are less likely to become resentful of you, since you aren't judging them as unacceptable or demanding that they change.

By choosing to influence rather than control, you accept and embrace the limits of what you can actually accomplish, as well as the limits of others. You respect others' autonomy and freedom to choose for themselves. This reflects your awareness that your influence may be great or small, immense or miniscule. Control, on the other hand, implies absolutes. If you control something, it does exactly what you want, whereas influence simply attempts to create an effect, no matter how small or how significant. You can't help but have some effect, some influence, on others. If you understand this as your goal, you can't fail.

Choosing influence over control is healthier for both yourself and others. When you choose to influence, you support the freedom of others to choose for themselves. You give them the permission that is crucial to creating extraordinary relationships. Maybe your attempts to influence will work, and maybe they won't. When they work, that's fantastic. When they don't, that's okay too. You can give permission completely nonetheless. The important thing is that you respect the freedom of others to be who they are and how they are and to make their own decisions about life, even regarding those aspects that directly affect you.

You have the ability to cultivate changes in yourself, others, and your relationships if you go about it in a healthy way. And as is now undoubtedly clear, the healthiest and most effective way is through choosing to influence. If you have any lingering doubts about this, the following lists will make the benefits of influence clear:

FOSTERING CHANGE THROUGH

Choosing to Influence	Attempting to Control
Understand and embrace the limits of your and others' abilities	Unable to see the limits of your and others' abilities
❄	❄
No expectation to change	Expect to successfully change
❄	❄
Not attached to outcome (might)	Attached to outcome (must)
❄	❄
Gives permission	Withholds permission
❄	❄
Respects autonomy	Increases codependence
❄	❄
Flexible posture (shades of gray; the middle way)	Absolute posture (black or white; all or nothing)
❄	❄
Supports freedom of choice	Denies freedom of choice
❄	❄
Cooperative and democratic	Autocratic and tyrannical
❄	❄
Intentionally cultivates harmony and calm in relationship	Unintentionally causes fight, flee, or freeze behaviors
❄	❄
Results in conversations	Results in conflicts
❄	❄
Invites others to grow closer	Pushes others away
❄	❄

38.
THE THREE RESPONSIBILITIES

Once you've given permission and are ready to start influencing change, you may wonder how to go about doing so. This is where the second truth about love comes in: the wisdom of taking responsibility. Specifically, you take responsibility for three things: your emotions, your communications, and your choices.

- **Taking responsibility for your emotions** means focusing on promoting harmony in yourself and your relationships through the art of giving permission.

- **Taking responsibility for your communications** means recognizing the power inherent in both verbal and nonverbal communication and exercising attention and care toward both.

- **Taking responsibility for your choices** means recognizing your own freedom and supporting the freedom of others. It means recognizing that the work of changing falls to you, rather than others. It means considering what you can do differently, not what others can do differently, and embracing your power to create the solutions you seek.

This is only a brief preview. The next three parts of the book will discuss each of these responsibilities extensively.

PART 4

TAKING RESPONSIBILITY FOR YOUR EMOTIONS

39.
"HARMONY PREPARES THE SOIL."

You may be in one or more relationships that aren't thriving as you wish. Maybe you and your partner are finding yourselves constantly arguing about the tiniest trifles. Maybe you don't talk to your mother on the phone as much as you used to because you're tired of her complaints. Maybe you've stopped spending time with someone who used to be a good friend. Maybe you have even written off some people because you feel that having a relationship with them simply isn't worth the trouble. If so, that's unfortunate because relationships are worth nurturing, even the challenging ones.

Nurturing a relationship is like tending a garden. If you neglect a garden, weeds will eventually overrun it and the flowers that once flourished will disappear. Luckily, no matter how run-down a garden is, with the right attention and care it can be brought back to life. The first step is to remove the obstacles: all the weeds and unwanted debris. Before growing something new, you first prepare the soil.

This is exactly how you can revitalize a relationship, as well. You start by removing the weeds (conflict), breaking up the compacted earth (old patterns of interacting), and smoothing out a level surface (a foundation of harmony). When you establish harmony by taking responsibility for your emotions, you ready the relationship for new growth.

Let's define harmony as a state of persistent and enduring calm within any relationship. When you get along well with someone, the relationship can be thought of as harmonious, and extraordinary relationships are abundant in harmony. My guess is that this is what you want: to feel at ease in relationships characterized by peace, serenity, and calm.

The calmer you are individually, the calmer your relationships will be. As such, to cultivate harmony in your relationships, aim to cultivate harmony within yourself by taking responsibility for your emotions. If someone gets upset at you, that's okay. Just give the person permission to be upset and focus on maintaining your own calm. Arguments erupt only when two people lose their calm. For the sake of your relationships, giving permission to others for their emotions will go a long way toward instilling harmony.

Of course, there's more to extraordinary relationships than harmony. Ultimately, the objective for our most valued relationships is intimacy—an experience of safety and closeness characterized by mutual feelings of affection and appreciation that occur in the absence of judgment. But intimacy can't be achieved in the absence of harmony, just like flowers won't blossom in nutrient-poor earth. Harmony is the soil of the garden; intimacy is the flowers and plants that emerge from it. Harmony precedes intimacy and therefore is the first waypoint on the journey toward any extraordinary relationship.

If you aim for intimacy without first achieving harmony, you won't succeed. Striving for intimacy before harmony leaves people highly reactive to much of what others say or do. They might feel hurt when their partner doesn't say, "I love you," or kiss them good-bye in the morning. This reactivity disrupts the relationship, diminishes harmony, and pushes the potential for intimacy farther away. The alternative is to take responsibility for your emotions, which honors the essential role of harmony in cultivating intimacy.

40.

"YOU ARE THE MASTER OF YOUR EMOTIONAL EXPERIENCE."

Especially in partner relationships, people generally hold fast to the belief that each is responsible for the emotions of the other. One person's feelings trigger feelings in the other, which then trigger feelings in the first. This makes the relationship look like a washing machine on spin cycle, with both people's emotions sloshing around one another like pieces of soapy, mismatched clothing, getting twisted into tighter and tighter tangles.

Remember that whenever you suffer, one thing is always true: you aren't giving permission. Of course, the same is true for others. When others are suffering, they aren't giving permission to something or someone—perhaps you. When that happens, you can give them permission for this too. There's no need to get upset or proclaim, "This has nothing to do with me. You're just creating your own suffering!" While that may indeed be true, it wouldn't be compassionate to say such a thing. The goal is to take responsibility, not dole it out.

If others don't know how to give permission or take responsibility for their emotions, you can give them permission for this as well. You can stay calm and keep doing whatever you can to promote harmony in the relationship. By taking responsibility for your emotions, you increase harmony within yourself, and that increases the amount of harmony in all of your relationships. You can do this entirely on your own when you take responsibility for your emotions by giving permission.

41.

"RELATIONSHIPS THRIVE ON EMOTIONAL AUTONOMY."

To be emotionally autonomous is to be in charge of your emotions. It's not about being unemotional. When a loved one dies, you will probably feel sad. There's nothing unhealthy or detrimental about feeling that way. Being emotionally autonomous simply means knowing why you feel the way you feel at any moment—the actual reason or reasons, not just the apparent ones. You take responsibility for your emotions, knowing that they are never caused by external things, including other people. You recognize that each emotion you experience comes from within you and, likewise, that each emotion others experience comes from within them. You let go of any belief that others make you feel how you feel or that others are obligated to think, feel, say, and do the "right things" to keep you free from suffering.

The greater your emotional autonomy, the less you will feel controlled by your environment. A buddha, or "enlightened one," manifests absolute emotional autonomy. There is nothing that you could do or say to a buddha that would elicit anger or frustration. Of course, you don't have to attain enlightenment to cultivate the emotional autonomy that will help you and your relationships suffer less. Just give permission.

Emotional autonomy is another waypoint on the path toward living more joyfully and experiencing greater harmony in your relationships as a result. It's an essential component of cultivating extraordinary relationships, and also one of the most essential means of taking responsibility for your emotions.

As your emotional autonomy grows, the spectrum of what others can think, feel, say, and do around you without you reacting and moving outside your emotional comfort zone will broaden. As you commit to giving permission with greater regularity, you'll notice that you get angry, irritated, and frustrated and feel hurt less often. In short, you'll become increasingly at ease with the world around you. This will become more effortless with time and practice.

The self-reliance of emotional autonomy also liberates you from the bonds of codependency. For the purposes of this book, let's define "codependency" as the opposite of emotional autonomy. By this definition, codependency is what occurs when people errone-ously believe that their emotional states are dictated by the actions and emotional states of others. Like most people, you've probably been strongly conditioned to be codependent; you can, however, retrain yourself by embracing emotional autonomy instead.

Emotional autonomy doesn't mean that you become indifferent to the emotions of others. You can still be compassionate and seek to increase their happiness. But you don't have to take responsibil-ity for others' emotions in order to help them. In fact, being emo-tionally autonomous is exactly how you can express your care for others and your relationships in the most loving way possible. After all, you can best help others by remaining calm and engaging them in constructive conversations that cultivate positive change. In contrast, those who are codependent often believe that they can best help themselves and others by fighting for change. But because fighting undermines harmony and weakens relationships, this approach never succeeds.

There's nothing coldhearted or selfish about being emotionally autonomous. In fact, the more emotional autonomy in a relation-ship, the more likely the relationship is to prosper. Why? Because, with emotional autonomy, you'll be able to embrace another per-son's upset without becoming upset yourself. Instead of getting pulled into the loop of doom, you can spare yourself and your partner from a conflict that would otherwise escalate and harm the relationship. Emotional autonomy is an act of compassion toward yourself, others, and all of your relationships.

42.

"AUTONOMY COMES FROM INTERNAL FRIENDSHIP."

The most important relationship you're in right now is with yourself. If you're unhappy, highly reactive, or codependent, it's likely that your relationship with yourself could use a little improvement. When you nurture your internal friendship, your emotional autonomy grows.

To improve your internal friendship, relate to yourself as you would relate to a child. Most people are instinctively kind, nurturing, and supportive toward children. We tend to extend a special kind of wisdom and compassion toward children that we may seldom offer to ourselves or other adults. Yet the ability to treat everyone this way is within us, so why not turn it inward, toward ourselves? In fact, as trite as this might sound, the truth is that there's a child within you that longs for your loving-kindness. The way to build internal friendship is to build an extraordinary relationship with this child.

There exists within you, simultaneously, two aspects of yourself. One part speaks; the other listens. The speaker is your mind, that verbal part of your consciousness that keeps a running commentary about you and your world. This is the voice that might call you fat, ugly, lazy, a failure, or whatever. It's a composite of the loudest voices you were exposed to as a child. Although these were most often the voices of your primary caregivers, others, such as teachers, schoolmates, or siblings, might have left an imprint too. To this day, we all tend to speak to ourselves much the way we were spoken to by important figures from our childhood. Our self-talk is the distant echo of their voices, still reverberating off our cranial walls these many years later. Our thoughts aren't really our own until we consciously set an intention to speak to ourselves in a new way—a way we choose. This is like internal parenting.

The truth is, you are always parenting the child within you. This child is the second part of you, the part that listens. Nothing you say to yourself falls on deaf ears; it falls on the ears of this child—your emotional self. The voice of the parent within you, your intellect, manifests in self-talk, which is fully absorbed by the child. When you are harsh or mean or judging, this soaks into your emotional self. The child doesn't know how to resist taking these messages personally. To the child, everything is personal. The child just listens without filters, takes everything in, and feels different ways about herself according to these messages.

Imagine saying to yourself something like *No one will ever love me* or *I'm a failure*. You may think that doesn't sound so bad. Perhaps it seems like you're merely sharing an opinion with yourself. Maybe you genuinely feel this way. But imagine yourself standing over a child, pointing a stern finger at her, and saying these same things: *No one will ever love you* or *You're a failure*. Sounds cruel, right?

Since your child part believes every word you tell her, choose to be nurturing and supportive. When your communication is kind, the child within experiences an increase of self-esteem, self-acceptance, and self-love. She learns that she isn't bad, wrong, or inadequate. She sees that she's okay just the way she is because you tell her so. As such, she continues to feel positive about herself and capable of anything. It is from this confidence, the confidence of your child, that your power emerges—the power to achieve anything you desire, the power, in fact, to change.

Instead of judging yourself, try giving permission. If you catch yourself thinking something like *No one will ever love me*, address your child in a different way, as a wise parent would. For instance, you might say, *I see how strongly you want to be in a loving relationship, and that's a beautiful thing. Because I believe in you and care about your happiness, I want you to know that I support you. Together, we can accomplish anything.* And this is true; with internal friendship, what you can accomplish becomes truly extraordinary.

43.

"INTERNAL FRIENDSHIP PREVENTS UNHEALTHY ATTACHMENT."

The stronger your internal friendship, the more confident you'll be in your ability to stand on your own two feet. This enables you to give permission to others with less fear of losing them, even if losing them is a very real possibility. You may give your partner permission to be who he is and, in so doing, discover that he doesn't want to continue the relationship, at least not romantically. Even if this isn't what you want, when your internal friendship is strong you can wish him success on his journey because you won't be emotionally attached in an unhealthy way. When the relationship ends well, this bodes well for your future relationships.

Unhealthy attachment is rigid, unyielding, and inflexible. To understand why it's problematic, imagine standing beside a large elephant and being attached to it by a metal rod. When the elephant charges at something, you get yanked along with it. When it goes left, you get dragged left. When it goes right, you get dragged right. This is unhealthy attachment—attachment that endangers you emotionally and strains your relationships.

Now imagine standing beside this same elephant, but this time you're attached to it by a mile-long rope with plenty of slack. If the elephant charges at something, you remain still. If it goes right or left, you aren't affected. This is healthy attachment. You can be attached to something or someone without it causing emotional turmoil or harming the relationship.

The key is to avoid rigid attachment—attachment dominated more by fear than fondness, more by needing than wanting, more by possessiveness than permissiveness. Any attachment that desires to limit the freedom of another is always a rigid attachment. With this type of attachment, you might insist that your partner go right when you go right, go left when you go left, run when you run, and stop when you stop. That might be fine for you, but how might your partner feel about this? Not so free, right? With rigid and fearful attachment, an extraordinary relationship built on harmony, respect, and intimacy is simply impossible.

Another consequence of rigid attachment is that, ironically, it actually prevents you from getting close to others and prevents others from getting close to you. Again think of the example with the elephant. If you're attached by the rod, not the rope, you can't get close enough to scratch the elephant behind his ears or give him a kiss on the forehead. With rigid attachment, you can't fully connect in an intimate way. But with the flexibility of the mile-long rope, you can.

One of the most loving things you can tell someone is actually "I don't need you." When said in a caring way, this shares your willingness to take responsibility for your own joyfulness and frees others to be fully themselves. It shows them that you give permission and that, as much as you love them, you do so in a way that's flexible and supportive.

Sabrina once attended a workshop for couples counselors and, after three hours of listening and synthesizing, her big takeaway was this: In any given moment, we make the choice to stay or leave a particular relationship. For the next few weeks, at the end of each day she asked herself whether she wanted to stay with her partner. She asked him to do the same, and later they compared notes. They agreed that if there was ever a time when either of them felt a desire to leave for days on end, they would investigate this with loving awareness. Twenty years have passed since then, and so far they have both agreed to stay. This is flexible attachment. This is love. It's the type of healthy attachment that's at the heart of extraordinary relationships.

44.
"YOU CAN BE INDEPENDENTLY JOYFUL."

Many people choose to endure romantic relationships marked by constant struggle instead of facing the potential discomforts of being alone. Fearful of solitude, they seem to be willing to stay in unfulfilling relationships indefinitely. Why? Because they don't know the truth: that they can be independently joyful.

If you lack confidence in your ability to be independently joyful, you may fear loneliness. Other fears may also compel you to endure an unfulfilling relationship: how others will judge you if the relationship ends, how getting a divorce might affect your children, whether you can support yourself financially, or whether you'll ever find someone who loves and cares for you better than your current partner, to name a few. However, fear is never a good reason to stay in a relationship.

The fact is, your joyfulness isn't dependent upon another person; it's dependent upon you. Actually, when it comes to romantic relationships, you have four options to choose from: you can (1) be joyful in a relationship; (2) be joyful alone; (3) suffer in a relationship; or (4) suffer alone.

Why would anyone choose suffering in a relationship over being joyful alone? You don't have to, not ever. Plus, if you're capable of being joyful alone, you'll be more capable of being joyful in a relationship. Either way, your joyfulness is what matters most. And your joyfulness is always possible when you take responsibility for your emotions.

45.

"PLUG INTO
MULTIPLE OUTLETS."

Knowing that you can be independently joyful doesn't mean you discount the importance of relationships to life satisfaction. The goal isn't to turn our backs on relationships; we just don't want to rely on any single relationship as our primary source of human connection.

Think of it like this: Everyone is like an appliance that requires energy to function. If you have just one cord, plugged into a single outlet, what happens if that cord gets unplugged? You quickly cease to function well. But if you have many cords plugged into many outlets, now what happens when one gets unplugged?

Obviously, it's safer to plug into multiple sources of emotional energy than just one. Instead of deriving your sense of joyfulness and worth from any single relationship, plug into multiple outlets. Dedicate time to all of your relationships, with friends both new and old, with family members, with coworkers or colleagues, and with yourself. You can fill your life with a wide variety of activities that are fun for you. You can nourish yourself with hobbies and passions, honoring and pursuing your wants. You can find work that feels meaningful to you. You can volunteer and give to others in ways that you enjoy. If you do these things, plugging into multiple outlets, you'll become more emotionally autonomous and independently joyful. As such, you'll be better able to fearlessly participate in your relationships.

46.
"FORAGING FOR JOY HELPS EVERYONE."

Imagine yourself as part of a village of hunter-gatherers. Each day, your task is to go out into the woods or jungle to bring back sustenance to share with the other members of your tribe. In this way, your individual efforts contribute to the well-being of the collective. Foraging for joy is very much like this.

I recently met with a client who felt that his wife's unhappiness was one of the biggest stressors his marriage faced on a daily basis. Noticing this, he began encouraging his wife to pursue her interests. Each time she did this, whether by going out for drinks with friends or attending a lecture with fellow professors, she brought home a little more joy to add to the marriage. It was as if she had gone into the woods and returned with a basket of nourishing berries for everyone.

If you pursue your own joy and give permission for others to pursue their own, this helps all members of the system. Whether your tribe has two people or ten, the efforts of each individual to forage for joy yield more abundance for sharing. Understanding this, allow yourself to go independently into the world to bring back some joy with you—joy that can be added to the feast—and encourage others to do the same. This is a fantastic way to enrich your relationships.

47.
REFLECTION POINT: RESPONSIBILITY FOR YOUR EMOTIONS

Before we move on to part 5, Taking Responsibility for Your Communications, let's review the main aspects of taking responsibility for your emotions:

- Know that all of your emotions come from you. Whenever you're upset, understand that this is because you aren't giving permission. Commit to managing this reaction by giving permission rather than acting out. This will promote harmony both within yourself and in your relationships. You can then better engage others in loving and supportive ways, which will help your relationships evolve and grow.

- Make internal friendship a priority and thereby increase your emotional autonomy. Emotional autonomy enhances your ability to love with flexibility and healthy attachment, genuinely supporting the freedom of others to be who they are. Remember that you can be independently joyful, and take responsibility for your individual joyfulness by plugging into multiple sources of emotional energy.

- Remember that the process of cultivating extraordinary relationships is about you and you alone. When you focus on your own ability to maintain harmony and enhance your joyfulness, you'll be more capable of engaging others with courage, authenticity, and loving-kindness.

PART 5

TAKING RESPONSIBILITY FOR YOUR COMMUNICATIONS

48.
"RELATIONSHIP IS COMMUNICATION."

You cannot relate to others (or yourself) without communication. Communication is any interaction in which something is exchanged between two or more entities. It is the means by which we interact with others, as well as how we interact with ourselves and the world around us. You don't have to be speaking to be communicating. When you sit silently beside your partner, you're still communicating—among other things, communicating that you feel comfortable enough with your partner to not fill your shared quietude with chatter.

As technology continues to connect us ever more quickly with one another, it becomes increasingly essential that we learn how to take responsibility for our communications. New connectivity tools not only seem to give us less time to think before speaking, but deprive us of the nonverbal cues that typically help us decipher the messages we receive, making it easier for misunderstandings to arise. This is all the more reason to master communicating in wise and responsible ways.

Relating well requires communicating well. When you take responsibility for your communications, you're taking responsibility for creating the types of relationships you desire—with your partner, others, yourself, and the world in general. As such, the process of cultivating extraordinary relationships relies heavily upon the "what" and "how" of communication. The chapters in this part of the book will offer you many tools to help you take responsibility for your communications in a refreshing new way.

49.
THE FIVE PRINCIPLES OF RESPONSIBLE COMMUNICATION

The list of characteristics that constitute effective communication may be endless. As such, I hesitate to suggest that there are only five principles of responsible communication. However, I have found that focusing on five particular principles helps people communicate in a way that promotes extraordinary relationships. These five principles are calm, objectivity, neutrality, inquiry, and cooperativeness. For now, don't worry about what each principle entails exactly. I'll cover all five in detail in the chapters that follow.

To remember this list, think of the word "iconic." Something that's iconic can symbolize a standard to aspire to. Responsible communication is a worthy standard, so the word "iconic" can serve as an acronym for the five principles, as in, "To take responsibility for my communications…

- I implement…

- Calm

- Objectivity

- Neutrality

- Inquiry

- Cooperativeness

If you like, write this on a small note card to carry with you to remind you of the five principles and encourage you to practice responsible communication in all your interactions.

50.
PRINCIPLE 1: CALM

Calm communicators tend to be adept communicators. Taking responsibility for your communications begins with taking responsibility for your emotions. When you're calm, you usually say what you mean to say and can better listen to others. In contrast, when you're emotionally outside your comfort zone and aren't calm, listening and speaking well can be difficult. For example, when in a reactive state, you might tell someone you love, "I hate you!" even though this is neither what you mean nor what you wish to say. You may also misinterpret things that are said to you. You may hear your partner say, "I hate you!" and fail to understand what she's really trying to convey, perhaps something more like, *My emotions are in an uproar right now, and I don't know how to handle this situation.* Being outside your comfort zone, you can't do this type of healthy interpreting for your partner.

When communicating, your top priority is to stay calm. Calm facilitates communication like nothing else can. When calm, you stand the best chance of communicating effectively. In this way, taking responsibility for your emotions allows you to start taking responsibility for your communications. One precedes the other. If you try to take responsibility for your communications without first taking responsibility for your emotions, it won't work out well. You can't communicate nearly as effectively while in a heightened emotional state. The next chapter explains why .

51.
"ADULTS DRIVE BETTER THAN CHILDREN."

Emotions are lovely. I'm not lobbying against emotions or being emotional. The goal isn't to be emotionless but to communicate your emotions effectively. There's nothing counterproductive about communicating your emotions in a healthy way, from within your comfort zone. But when you don't speak from a calm space, you probably end up communicating more like a child or a rebellious teen than a mature adult. Indeed, as discussed in chapter 42, emotions are very much like children.

Think of it like this: Your mind, your capacity to reason and articulate thoughts through language, is like a responsible parent driving a car. You are the car, and your mind guides you through life. It obeys stoplights and road signs and maintains a steady course within the legal speed limit. It knows how to drive, and as long as it commands the wheel, you don't crash. However, in the backseat sits a child—your emotions. This child sometimes sits quietly, content to stare out the window at passing scenery. Other times, however, he feels compelled to whine, cry, or scream to get the adult's attention about something.

When your emotions exceed your comfort zone, what typically happens is akin to the parent letting the child get in the front seat and start driving the car. The likely result is that the car swerves, veers, and randomly starts and stops with abrupt and unnerving jerks until it spins out of control, flips, and rolls a few times. Of course, this really pisses off or scares any other drivers on the road.

Who's responsible for the crash? Not the child, of course. The child can't see over the dashboard and has no driving experience and therefore cannot be expected to drive well. The parent is responsible because of handing the controls over to the child in the first place.

Even the wisest of us occasionally find that our child (our emotions) has grabbed the steering wheel while we weren't paying attention. Since you're human, you're bound to get upset once in a while. Sometimes you'll get upset in an instant; other times it may happen more gradually. Whether your child leaps into the front seat in an instant or crawls there slowly, your job is always the same: to notice this as soon as possible and tenderly intervene.

You can avoid having your child take control by paying attention to him. Whenever you start feeling upset, recognize that your child is the one upset, not you. He's unbuckling his seat belt. If you notice this early on, you can preempt the takeover: "Ah, I know where you're heading," you say to your child. "You can relax and trust me to attend to this. You're in good hands, I promise." With compassion, you give your child permission to feel upset, while also giving permission to whatever seemingly sparked his reaction (which is your reaction too). In this way, you step in before your child takes the wheel.

Communication is how you express yourself and shape your relationships. If you communicate with calm and intentionality, you can arrive at your destinations safely. You can listen to your child (your emotions), along the way; you just don't want him to do the driving.

52.

"EARLY COMMUNICATION IS EASY COMMUNICATION."

Most conflicts in relationships occur because something that could have been talked about sooner went ignored for too long. Whatever it is, one or both people allowed the issue to fester under the surface, not wanting to address it. Ironically, this choice is usually made in an effort to promote harmony in the relationship. Unfortunately, emotion about this issue continues to grow to the point where it can no longer be contained and then, apparently all of a sudden, there's an explosive conflict. What once could have been discussed calmly becomes an emotionally charged argument in which little can be accomplished. The solution to this is to choose early communication.

The calmer you are, the easier your communications will be. Realizing this, you can choose to address issues as they arise, while you are only a bit outside your comfort zone or, better yet, when you notice yourself nearing its edge. Since you aren't overly emotional at that time, you increase your chances of communicating about the issue in a way that facilitates arriving at a solution while protecting the relationship from unnecessary disharmony.

Choosing early communication over late communication is the act of choosing easy communication over difficult communication. That's a smart choice! Although it may take some courage to address a matter early on, doing so extends compassion to both yourself and others. It spares your relationships from bigger and more difficult confrontations in the future.

53.

"GIVING PERMISSION IS NOT ABOUT KEEPING YOUR MOUTH SHUT."

Giving permission isn't about keeping your mouth shut or ignoring things; it's about managing your emotions and behaviors so you can communicate effectively whenever you choose. If you don't address something that concerns you because you want to give permission, you might end up only imitating giving permission. Let's look at an example.

Let's say you notice a pattern of your partner leaving his clothes on the floor. Although you feel annoyed, you decide not to mention it because you don't want to henpeck or come across as judgmental. So you button your lips, aspiring to give permission instead. You let the clothes accumulate, or you put them in the hamper yourself. However, every time you see more clothes on the floor, you recognize that you're feeling a bit more annoyed. Yet still you say nothing, trying to be permissive, trying to embrace your partner 100 percent. As the clothes continue to pile up, your resentment and annoyance grow. Eventually, you can't take it anymore. Your emotion reaches a tipping point. You see one more piece of clothing on the floor, and it's simply too much to bear. Then you erupt: "Will you for once just put your clothes in the damn hamper?"

How is your partner likely to react to this? Chances are, your outburst will catch him completely off guard. He might lash out, "What's your problem?" You may then find yourself quickly racing into the loop of doom. Bummer. Why did this happen?

It happened because you were never actually giving permission. How do you know this? In retrospect, you can see that your annoyance persisted and, in fact, grew. When you give permission successfully, your emotions transform. Whenever you attempt to give permission but are unsuccessful, your unwanted emotions persist. This is a cue to open your mouth and mention your concern. Out of compassion for the relationship, knowing that conversations are easier than arguments, speak up. You protect the relationship not by holding your tongue, but by communicating.

When you find yourself reacting, take responsibility for your emotions by giving permission. If your annoyance persists, consider whether there's something about the situation that you genuinely have difficulty giving permission for, even if only something small. Ideally, you'll eventually be able to give permission for anything, but for now, you're likely to hit a snag every once in a while. That's okay. The important thing is to notice when an attempt to give permission isn't working.

In the example above, after continuing to feel annoyed for a while, you could have chosen to bring the topic up for discussion early on, rather than waiting. You might have said, in a completely calm way, "I have this thing about tidiness and would love it if you would be willing to put your clothes in the hamper instead of leaving them on the floor. That would show me that you appreciate the work I do to keep our house clean." Note the absence of judgment, ridicule, or complaint in this statement. It is purely information about yourself that you're sharing with your partner. Not only will your partner appreciate being spoken to in this mature way, he'll also be more receptive to what you're sharing and, in all likelihood, will change his behavior accordingly. Through communication, the relationship grows.

54.

"CONFLICT AVOIDANCE DOES NOT AVOID CONFLICT."

Many people choose not to confront their partner about concerns because they don't want to rock the boat. Here's the thing, though: Boats are designed to rock, designed to steadily move up and down, right and left, along with each current and wave. In fact, this is what keeps them stable. The same is true for relationships. A healthy relationship is one that is allowed to rock gently and gracefully with each current and wave. Relationships can handle this. What they may not be able to handle is refusal to let them rock a bit. Actually, a boat that doesn't rock is bound to capsize in high seas. This probably isn't what you want.

True stability is achieved through flexibility. Which is stronger, stone or water? Which is more likely to withstand the force of a powerful blow without being harmed? In a strong wind, a mighty oak might topple while bamboo bends. Buildings retrofitted to withstand earthquakes are designed to sway, as are expansive bridges. If you want your relationships to be stable, allow them to sway. If you want to avoid conflict, remain open to the *possibility* of conflict so you can address issues early on. Trust that, using the tools in this book, you have the ability to communicate well about anything, even in the event that emotions escalate. Embracing this ability, you can become less fearful of conflict and more willing to face issues directly as they arise.

Actually, trying to avoid conflict isn't such a bad thing. I don't want conflict in my life either. Who does? Just understand that the sensible way to avoid conflict entails willingness to communicate early on. Besides, there's a big difference between conversation and conflict. Conversation, in the form of mature dialogue, occurs on the back of emotional ripples, whereas conflict occurs on the back of tsunamis. To avoid conflict, allow your relationships to ride upon the smaller, gentler waves. Why? Because smaller waves are always less likely to capsize your boat.

Confronting others in a mature way takes courage, but it takes compassion too. If you shy away from difficult conversations, you'll eventually encounter a conflict that can harm you, the other person, and the relationship you were trying to protect. If you're afraid to speak your mind or afraid that someone will react to you in a way that you don't want, no matter how calm your approach, you're setting the stage for an even greater confrontation in the future. Instead, embrace your ability to give permission to others to react however they are going to react when you try to communicate with them. And the truth is, no matter how calmly you communicate, the other person may react strongly in response. That's okay. You can give permission for this while also taking responsibility for your own emotions and communication. In this way, you avoid the tsunami.

Trusting that you can manage your emotions and let others manage theirs will help you maintain willingness to address issues when they occur or when you notice a developing pattern. And by remaining calm, you can prevent conversations from becoming conflicts. Although this isn't always easy, it is always true. A conflict occurs only when *two* people are outside of their comfort zone. As such, staying within your comfort zone is, without question, the most surefire way to avoid conflict during any interaction.

55.

"APPROACH IS NOT CONFRONTATION."

If you are fearful of confronting others, try approaching instead. What's the difference? When you confront, there is usually some expectation that conflict will follow. Approaching is not like this. Approaching is loving and calm, spares others from feeling judged, shares information in a gentle way, and invites conversation. The following examples may help you consider ways to approach the important people in your life:

- **To a partner:** "I've noticed your interest in watching TV on our date nights. I enjoy that, and lately I also notice how I miss the times when we'd go out on the deck, light a fire, and listen to music. Do you feel the same way?"

- **To a child:** "I notice you aren't spending as much time studying recently. I've been thinking that you've given up on your dreams. Is there any truth to this? If not, can I support you in a way I haven't been? Maybe your dreams have changed. If so, I want you to know that, no matter what, I love you and I have your back."

- **To a parent:** "Mom, about five minutes ago, you asked how I was doing, and then you continued to talk about yourself. I notice that I shut down when this happens. I want us to be close, so I was wondering if I could share what has been going on with me also. How would that be?"

56.
PRINCIPLE 2: OBJECTIVITY

What is the opposite of negativity? Positivity? Nope! Negativity and positivity are actually quite similar: both are subjective and judgmental, and both are a matter of opinion. The true opposite of negativity is objectivity. It's not only the opposite of negativity, but also its antidote.

Objective language is truthful. Truthfulness, however, is different than honesty. For instance, you might tell your partner, "You really hurt my feelings." You genuinely think this, so you're being honest. But are you being truthful? No. The truth is, you didn't give permission for your partner to do whatever she did or say whatever she said, and *that's* what hurt your feelings. So you can see, being objective is not necessarily an easy task. It requires the wisdom to discern truth from fiction. If you're speaking truthfully, you're being objective and taking responsibility for your communications.

Let's define "objectivity" as a perspective that is inarguably true. Communicating in this way minimizes the likelihood of disagreement. After all, you are only sharing a truth. As such, there is nothing for another person (or yourself) to argue against. Great! You can then have a conversation instead—one that sticks to the facts, promotes harmony, and facilitates change. Of course, there is much more that constitutes objectivity, and I'll turn to that topic soon. For now, just understand that remaining inarguably truthful in your communications, in both your speech and your thoughts, achieves wonders.

57.
"EMBRACE THE POWER OF 'MAYBE.'"

One Zen story clearly conveys the wisdom of objectivity. Once upon a time, there was an old farmer whose horse ran away. "Such misfortune," consoled his neighbors. "Maybe yes, maybe no," the farmer replied. The next day the horse returned, along with four wild horses. "How fantastic!" the neighbors exclaimed. "Maybe yes, maybe no," replied the old man. The next day, his son hopped onto one of the untamed steeds, was thrown, and broke his leg. The neighbors again offered their sympathy for his bad luck. "Maybe yes, maybe no," answered the farmer. The following day, the military came to the village to draft new soldiers. Seeing that the son was injured, they passed him by. The neighbors congratulated the farmer on his good fortune. "Maybe yes, maybe no," said the farmer. "Maybe" asserts wisdom—wisdom that remains grounded in truth rather than getting lost in subjective ideas and judgments about what is and is not so.

"Maybe" is on my list of favorite words. It can quickly create objectivity and add truthfulness. The small nudge it gives is enough to help you start transforming false thinking and speech toward objectivity. Let's see how this might work with negative self-talk.

No matter what your self-judgment is, perhaps *I'm ugly*, *I'm a loser*, or *I'm fat*, you can simply add the phrase "or maybe I'm not." That changes everything. By adding this phrase, you challenge the veracity of your opinion without forcing yourself into believing something different—something you may not believe. You create a bit of wiggle room that allows your thinking to shift. "Or maybe I'm not" awakens you to the possibility that you could be totally wrong. *That's* being objective.

With any negative (false) statement or self-talk, you can always create more truthfulness and objectivity by employing the word "maybe." Doing so will help you relinquish judgments. Indeed, maybe you are wrong. Once you embrace this possibility, thinking that was once concrete and unassailable becomes more fluid and malleable. Once something is malleable, it can be reshaped. This is how you can transform negativity—by cultivating objectivity.

This approach is equally valuable when you catch yourself judging others. You can add a little more objectivity by reminding yourself that maybe you're wrong. This is always true. You could always be wrong. In fact, it could be said that the very nature of judging means that all judgments are wrong.

Here are some examples of how you can relate to yourself and others with greater truthfulness and accuracy, creating objectivity by using the word "maybe":

- **Toward yourself:**
  - "I'm lazy...*or maybe I'm not*. Maybe I'm just not feeling motivated right now."
  - "I'm going to fail...*or maybe I won't*. Maybe I'll do just fine."
  - "I'll never find a partner...*or maybe I will*. Maybe I've just been looking for relationships in a way that hasn't been working for me."

- **Toward others:**
  - "Jennifer is mean...*or maybe she isn't*. Maybe she's just having a bad day."
  - "Richard is selfish...*or maybe he isn't*. Maybe he just doesn't know how to be generous."

- **Toward circumstances:**
  - "My job sucks...*or maybe it doesn't*. Maybe I just don't feel challenged."
  - "This car is a piece of junk...*or maybe it isn't*. Maybe it could just use a little work to help it run better."

58.
"THERE ARE NO NEEDS."

One of the most common ways people fail to be objective is with the word "need." Indeed, most people employ this word many times each day. I need to go to the grocery store. I need to pay the phone bill. I need to feed the dogs. I need a vacation. You need to take the trash out. You need to learn how to listen. Unfortunately, all of these statements are false. Why? Because none of them are objective—none are inarguably true. The inarguable truth is that you (and others) don't *need* anything or need to do anything. Additionally, there is nothing that you need from others, nor anything that others need from you. Seem untrue? I invite you to convince me of one thing that you need.

You might say you absolutely need air. Actually, you don't. True, without air you'll die, but you don't *need* to not die. You can die if you want. You can choose to not breathe if you want. Of course, if you're successful in not breathing, the likely result is that you'll lose consciousness and your body will resume breathing. Still, you understand the point. Likewise, you don't *need* food, love or affection, more free time, or more money. You may want these things, but you don't need them. You don't need anything.

Whenever you use the word "need," you're not being objective. The exception is when "need" follows a conditional statement, such as "In order to live, I need air." Whenever you say that you need something in the absence of a conditional statement, you're lying. It's just not true. Perhaps this seems like splitting hairs. Maybe you're thinking, *Come on, this is semantics.* The thing is, the precise words we use to communicate are relevant because they are extremely powerful. "Need" in particular is a tremendously powerful word, and by using it, we actually harm ourselves and our relationships in a very specific way.

The word "need" is actually one of the most toxic words out there, not only because it's typically false, but because it actually diminishes the likelihood that we will get whatever we think we need. Here's why: When you were a child, you were probably often told what you needed to do. You "needed" to clean your room, get better grades, stop running in the house, get home by nine o'clock, and on and on. How did you react to this? You probably cringed. You probably didn't like being commanded to do this or that. In fact, you probably resisted doing whatever you were told you needed to do, especially as you grew older and more independent. More and more, you wanted to rebel and deliberately not do those things, just to assert your individuality and freedom. No one likes to be told what they need to do—not children, and not adults.

Actually, children are fairly smart. When children are told that they need to do something, they resist—not so much because they are stubborn, but because they know better. They know it's not true; they know that they don't *need* to clean their room or do their homework, or anything else for that matter. That's why children commonly roll their eyes at such ludicrous commandments. They realize that they're being hustled and, as a result, they resist.

When you tell yourself what you need to do, the legacy of your childhood experience surfaces and part of you reacts as you did when you were young. Part of you wants to resist and often does. Sure, you might do whatever you're telling yourself you need to do, but probably not with a smile on your face. You'll do it begrudgingly—or not do it at all. The language of need doesn't work. It makes you less likely, not more likely, to do something.

One expedient way to cultivate objectivity is to stop telling yourself what you need to think, feel, say, or do—and to stop telling others these same things. Whenever you catch yourself using the word "need," recognize that you aren't being objective and replace the word "need" with either "want" or "don't want." Indeed, whatever you're telling yourself you need is always something you either want or don't want. And, whereas "need" is always false, "want" or "don't want" is always true, provided you truly understand your genuine goals and desires. For example, "I need to go to the gym" (false) becomes either "I want to go to the gym" or "I don't want to go to the gym." One of these two statements will be true.

This is also a good way to take responsibility for your communications, replacing a false statement with a true one. When you realize that what you think you need is actually something you want and tell yourself, "I want to go to the gym," rather than "I need to go to the gym," then you'll feel different about going to the gym. You'll feel motivated rather than demotivated. You'll be reminded of your willingness to do this thing because it's your choice and not your obligation.

Of course, sometimes when you examine your use of the word "need," you might find that you've used it to indicate something you don't want. For instance, "I need to go to the dentist" might become "I don't want to go to the dentist." Fine. If you don't want to go to the dentist, you can give yourself permission not to go. Of course, it can get complicated. You might say, "But I have a toothache that's killing me!" So in that case, what are you really saying? Maybe you want to go to the dentist because you want your tooth to feel better. If that's what you want, you can give yourself permission for that too. Identifying this as something you want (even if at first it seems like something you don't want) encourages you to go ahead and do it.

What about those "needs" that simply stay "don't wants"? For example, you might tell yourself, *I need to change the oil in my wife's car.* You know that's not true, because there are no needs. So, what is true? Do you want to personally attend to the maintenance of your wife's car? If the answer is no, then you can give yourself permission to take it to a mechanic instead or ask her to.

"Need" language tends to heighten emotion. If you don't get something you think you need, you're obviously more likely to fret about it. This creates more suffering, both for yourself and for others. On the other hand, if you don't get something you *want*, you're more likely to feel that it isn't as big a deal. "Need" language unnecessarily ups the stakes, and this can lead to emotional reactions that undermine relationships.

Try to avoid "need" language in your communications with others. Telling people what they need to do or what you need from them is false and counterproductive. Choose to be factual and truthful instead. If you want to tell others what you want them to do, okay. That's good information for them; for example, "I want you to help me change the sheets this morning. Would you be willing to do this?" Asking for someone's willingness to participate in what you want frees them to make their own choice. That's very liberating!

When you tell others what they need to do, you disrespect their freedom to live a life of their choosing and actually discourage them from giving whatever it is you want. This creates disharmony and injures relationships. When you tell yourself what you need to do or how you need to be, you're committing this same injustice and harming your internal friendship. In truth, you are allowed to be who you are, exactly as you are, and don't *need* to be otherwise. You deserve to give yourself this permission. Likewise, others are allowed to be who they are, exactly as they are, and don't need to be otherwise. When you understand and embrace this, everyone wins.

Over the course of the next week, see how many times you use the word "need" in a way that isn't objective. It will probably be often, and that's okay. Also try substituting either "want" or "don't want" and see what happens. Notice how different you feel when you think and speak with "want" language instead of "need" language. Notice how others respond to you differently when you speak to them in terms of what you want rather than what you need. You'll be amazed at the comparison.

59.
"THERE ARE NO 'SHOULDS.'"

"Should" language is similar to "need" language. Whereas "need" is always false, "should" is always subjective and therefore never truthful or objective. Who determines what you should or should not do? Your parents? Society? Friends? Your lover? Your religion? "Shoulds" are always a matter of opinion. "Should" presupposes that there is a right or wrong thing to think, feel, say, or do—a right or wrong way to be. That's just not true. In reality, there are no "shoulds."

As with "need," you can translate "should" statements into either "want" or "don't want." Instead of thinking, *I should buy flowers for my partner,* ask yourself if you actually *want* to make this gesture. If you do, recognizing this will inspire you to do so gladly, knowing you have this freedom. If you don't want to, then let yourself communicate your affection or appreciation a different way, also gladly. You could tell yourself, *I don't want to spend money on flowers that will only last a few days. Since I want my partner to know how I feel, what am I willing to do instead to express myself?* This way, there's no guilt or resentment from feeling like you were forced to do something. The truth is, there's nothing you should do and no way you should be. Embrace this freedom.

Just as with "need" language, by avoiding "should" language you go a bit further toward cultivating objectivity. You, others, and your relationships will benefit immensely from this.

60.
PRINCIPLE 3: NEUTRALITY

Aikido is a unique martial art designed to protect both oneself and an aggressor at the same time. Aikido masters never strike out at an opponent, and when attacked, they counter the aggression with minimal effort by redirecting the opponent's own force in a way that minimizes harm to both individuals. The third principle of responsible communication, maintaining the balance of neutrality, is exactly like this.

When communicating, face others confidently, remain calm, communicate what you want to say, and listen to what others have to say to you. When you take responsibility for your communications by practicing neutrality, you commit to being neither aggressive nor defensive in your speech—no attacking, no defending. Why? Because attacking and defending are tactics used in combat. Since combat probably isn't what you want in your relationships, aim for neutrality instead.

We all know aggression and defensiveness when we hear them. We know when we're attacking, and we know when we're being defensive. Neither stance is effective for promoting extraordinary relationships because both occur while we are outside our emotional comfort zone. Both are forms of acting out, and as such, both undermine harmony and injure relationships. Strive to remain neutral—neither aggressive nor defensive. The next two chapters take a closer look at aggression and defensiveness and the effect they have on relationships.

61.

"THERE'S NEVER A GOOD
REASON TO AGGRESS."

Morihei Ueshiba, the creator of aikido, maintained that injuring an opponent is injuring oneself, and that controlling aggression and not inflicting injury is the art of peace. Aggression is never the answer. If you want to practice the art of peace, which is a hallmark of extraordinary relationships, understand that there's never a good reason to aggress.

In terms of communication, aggression shows up as attacks on others or judging them as somehow bad or wrong. By now you know how detrimental this can be. Aggression pushes others away and teaches them that you don't value and appreciate them as they are, even if this isn't your intention. In this way, aggression always injures relationships.

You don't have to judge others or call people out on things you don't like or things you want to see changed. You can always say whatever you want to say in a way that protects relationships. For instance, you don't have to call someone a slob to inspire cleanliness, don't have to call someone fat to inspire health, and don't have to call someone selfish to inspire caring. In fact, quite the opposite.

Aggression tends to worsen the situation because it worsens relationships. If you call someone a slob, what motivation will she have to be tidier? If you call someone fat, he'll probably just feel worse about himself and less motivated to lose weight. If you call someone selfish, she's going to feel less inclined to act tenderly toward you. Simply put, aggression backfires. It doesn't inspire change.

Instead of aggressing, converse. Share that you want or would appreciate more tidiness, a healthier partner, or more tenderness.

Offer this information about yourself in a way that isn't aggressive. Instead of judging others as bad or wrong, consider trying to discover what makes the problematic behavior flourish. You may learn that your girlfriend is ashamed to admit that her mother is a hoarder and that, having grown up in such a household, to her, having just a few mislaid items is a major accomplishment. This allows you to appreciate her current efforts and ask if you can help in some way.

Likewise, after meeting your boyfriend's parents, you might realize that his family considers heftiness manly, almost a point of pride. Instead of combating this, you can help your partner define his masculinity in ways that don't threaten his health, because you love him and want him to be around for a long while.

Or instead of criticizing your girlfriend's selfishness, you might ask her how she expresses her affection for you. To her, maybe leaving you alone is a way of caring because she thinks this is what you want. Perhaps she had no idea you wanted to snuggle more. Conversation that occurs in the presence of understanding and absence of aggression allows this information to come to light.

When taking responsibility for your communications, the goal is always to engage others in constructive conversations in which relevant and useful information can be exchanged. Aggression doesn't have a place in this. It interferes with the exchange that is otherwise possible through calm, objective, and neutral conversation.

62.
"THERE'S NEVER A GOOD REASON TO DEFEND YOURSELF."

When I say, "There's never a good reason to defend yourself," I am of course not talking about physical self-defense. So let me rephrase that: in communication, there's never a good reason to defend yourself. Why? Because you're never being attacked. People are allowed to think whatever they think, feel whatever they feel, say whatever they say, and do whatever they do. That they do so isn't a personal matter. If you get defensive, you're making something that isn't personal into a personal matter; you're making something that's completely about another person into something about you.

You can let people think whatever they think, even if you know it isn't true. In fact, the more obviously untrue something is, the easier it is not to get defensive. For instance, imagine someone calls you a yellow lunch box. Well, that's absurd. You know you're not a yellow lunch box, and chances are, you don't get the least bit defensive at the assertion of such a ridiculous claim because you know it's false.

Now imagine that someone calls you a failure, selfish, or a nag. That's a whole other story! You contemplate whether this is true. Maybe you're not sure. Maybe there's some small measure of truth in it, something to learn about yourself. In fact, the more you might agree with a claim or at least suspect there may be some truth in it, the more likely you are to react with defensiveness. Ironically, we tend to argue more vehemently against the things we think may hold some truth than those we know are false. Regardless, no matter how much or how little truth might exist in a statement, getting defensive is never the answer. Defensiveness only creates more suffering for ourselves, suffering that generally leads to the loop of doom.

Defensiveness, like aggression, is a form of acting out that comes from emotional reaction. When you're defensive, you're speaking, not listening. You're fighting against what the other person has to say. But the truth is, you never need to change someone's opinion, even if your own is different. You don't need to prove yourself right or get others to think as you think. By not getting defensive, you show others that their opinion has value.

Recognizing that everyone is entitled to their own opinion allows you to discover more about why others have the opinions they express. You can let their opinions be what they are, neither right nor wrong, neither good nor bad. If you don't get defensive and simply ask about the person's opinion, this is highly validating; it's like saying, "I accept you and your opinion. I care what you have to say and want to learn more about you. I'm listening." From this, a conversation can flow.

Still, it can be difficult to not get defensive, especially if doing so is habitual. The first thing to do is simply notice your defensiveness when it arises and see it as a signal that you're outside of your emotional comfort zone. As such, the solution is the same as always: give permission. Realize that the other person is simply sharing an opinion with you, and that's okay. Open yourself up to what is being shared, understanding that whatever anyone says is merely information about that person, not about you. Remain calm and investigate the opinion further by engaging the person in a conversation about it. When you resist the temptation to defend yourself, you remain receptive. The other person will then feel heard, and the relationship will probably strengthen because of the healthy exchange that follows. Maintaining neutrality is invaluable for communicating in a way that fosters extraordinary relationships.

63.
PRINCIPLE 4: INQUIRY

The first three principles of responsible communication—calm, objectivity, and neutrality—serve as guidelines for the process of healthy communication. The fourth principle, inquiry, addresses content.

The principle of inquiry is a reminder to ask questions. Questions are by far the most powerful communication tool at your disposal. A thoughtful question can steer a conversation in any direction you choose. Of course, not all questions achieve this.

Questions that cultivate extraordinary relationships are fueled by a spirit of curiosity and a sincere desire to nonjudgmentally understand others for who they are. Ask questions because you want to learn more. When someone says or does something you don't like, instead of getting upset or acting out, give permission, return to your comfort zone, and then become curious. Next, ask a question.

The truth is, everyone is always changing. In fact, you are no longer the same person you were when you started reading this chapter. You're similar, but you aren't the same. Curiosity opens the door to discovering others for who and how they are in each new moment. Inquiry is how you seek to satisfy your curiosity, knowing that the more you learn about others, the deeper your relationships with them can become.

64.
"ONE PLUS ONE DOES NOT EQUAL TWO."

What if you and I were to attempt to have a conversation in which I'm talking about the Philadelphia Eagles and you're talking about the merits of vegetarianism? That wouldn't go too well, would it? And why? Because a monologue (one) plus a monologue (one) never equals a dialogue (two). True conversations are dialogues. Unfortunately, many people think they're having conversations when they're actually taking turns monologuing.

Communication breaks down when both participants aren't listening to what the other is saying. One person has something to say and says it, then the other person has something to say and says it. Each is usually so busy trying to be heard and understood that a logjam of words clogs the channels of communication. All too often, one person speaks her mind, awaits a reply, evaluates whether the other person has understood her, and then, deeming from the person's response that he hasn't, reiterates herself. Of course, the other person is usually doing the same thing. Let's look at an example:

"You shouldn't have hung up on me. That was so rude."

"All you were doing was yelling at me. I couldn't take it anymore."

"I wasn't yelling. You're totally exaggerating."

"You were too yelling. And it was getting annoying. I don't have to put up with that."

This isn't a dialogue; it's two monologues. Although it appears that both people are talking about the same topic—how their latest telephone conversation ended—each is actually discussing something different: namely, his or her own perspective. It's not one topic, but two.

In the above example, the first person presents a topic for conversation: her thought that it was rude for her partner to have hung up on her. They could have a constructive conversation about this if they stay on topic, but this doesn't happen. Instead, the second person presents a new topic: that he's sick of being yelled at. Because there are two topics, the conversation gets stuck. Now let's look at what might happen if the second person stays on topic, rather than introducing something new:

"You shouldn't have hung up on me. That was so rude."

"You didn't want me to hang up on you?"

"Of course not. I was in the middle of saying something."

"And you think that hanging up on you was rude?"

"Definitely. How are we going to improve our relationship if all you do is run away every time things don't go well."

"So that's what you want? You want our relationship to improve?"

"Absolutely."

"Me too!"

Here, the second person doesn't try to change his partner's mind about hanging up being rude. He doesn't get defensive or argue. He gives permission instead and stays on topic by asking questions. This creates a conversation. If this dialogue were to continue in this way, the two participants could segue into a deeper discussion about how to improve their relationship. Ideally, each would ask questions of the other, allowing them to grow closer without a struggle.

Whenever you're confronted by an emotional outburst, complaint, or criticism from another person, begin a dialogue. If you find yourself reacting emotionally and feel an immediate urge to explain or defend yourself, resist the temptation. Instead, give permission; this will reduce your emotional reaction and facilitate communication. Instead of sharing your opinion, initiate a conversation by asking questions.

65.

"QUESTIONS OPEN DOORS TO CONVERSATION."

There's a big difference between statements and questions. Statements send information outward; questions invite information inward. When you ask genuine questions, you open a door and invite the words of another person to enter into you. You give the thoughts and feelings of the other person a place to go. This promotes healthy dialogue. Just keep in mind that not all questions are true questions. For instance, "What the hell were you thinking?" isn't a question; it's a statement that basically says something like "You shouldn't have done that!" A question mark at the end of a sentence doesn't always make it a question.

A beautiful consequence of asking true questions is that people seldom react to them with defensiveness. A genuine question isn't an attack, so people feel less compelled to defend themselves in response, providing your tone isn't aggressive. When someone says something to you, even something you disagree with or believe to be inaccurate, try responding with a question, rather than giving in to the all-too-common impulse to offer a rebuttal.

For example, imagine that your partner calls you a selfish, irresponsible jerk. Assuming you disagree, your instinct is probably to debate this opinion, perhaps saying something like "I am not!" You don't want your partner to think of you like this, so you try to change her mind.

However, this approach almost always leads to conflict. Instead, give permission for your partner to think what she thinks and ask a question such as, "Okay, what makes you think so?" This is neither agreement nor disagreement, and it protects the relationship. After all, the statement that you're a selfish, irresponsible jerk is only personal perspective, but because it is this person's perspective, it has value, whether it's true or not. The goal, therefore, is to find out more about why your partner has this opinion. There are bound to be reasons, and once you discover them, her statement will make more sense.

Imagine a woman telling her husband something like "All you ever think about is work. You never have any time for me. You don't even care about me anymore." The husband's instinctive response to such a statement might be "That's nonsense; I don't only think about work" or "Give me a break! Who do you think pays for this nice house we live in?" or "How many times do I have to tell you: I do care about you; it's just that I can't afford to not care about work also." In each of these replies, the husband counters his wife's viewpoint by expressing his own. Even if his goal is to mollify his wife, sharing his viewpoint closes the doors of communication. At best, it will accomplish nothing; at worst, it could precipitate a full-blown argument.

By responding to his wife's statement with another statement, the husband essentially ignores his wife's perspective, which invalidates it. Why? Because he disagrees. He thinks her statement is unfair and untrue. After all, he knows he doesn't only care about work. He loves his wife and wishes she wouldn't question his love. His work simply demands a great deal of his attention. He wishes she would understand this and not give him such a hard time. He's doing the best he can. Unfortunately, he's focused on defending himself. Could this budding argument be averted if he were to ask questions instead? You bet.

Now let's imagine that this woman confronts her husband, again with the statement, "All you ever think about is work. You never have any time for me. You don't even care about me anymore." This time, let's say the husband takes responsibility for his communication through inquiry. Because he embraces the power of asking questions, he replies, "What makes you think that the only thing I ever think about is work?" Here's how the conversation might unfold:

"Because that's all you do. You come home and work until it's time for bed. We never get to spend any time together."

"And that's what you want? You want us to spend more time together?"

"Of course I do. Don't you?"

"Absolutely. I feel the same way. I wish work wasn't so demanding right now."

"I just miss you, that's all."

"I miss you too. And maybe you're right. Maybe I can afford to take a little break. Is there something you'd like to do together right now?"

"Can we just sit here and give each other foot massages and talk? I'd really like that."

"Definitely. I'd like that too."

That is so much more productive. Of course, an idealized fictional dialogue is one thing, and real life another. Still, give this approach a try. When you next find yourself in an argument of some kind, realize that communication has gotten stuck. To transform this impasse, invite the other person to join you in a conversation instead by asking a question. Here are some examples:

- "What is it that you want me to know right now?"

- "Is there something you want me to do differently in the future?"

- "Is there something that you're hoping to hear from me right now?"

- "Do you have any ideas about how we can remedy this situation?"

Questions move the interaction toward conversation, creating an opportunity for each person to learn about the other and for both to grow together toward a more extraordinary relationship.

66.
"QUESTIONS GUIDE CONVERSATIONS."

Just as you can think of yourself as having 99 percent control of your relationships, you can think of yourself as having 99 percent control of your conversations. You can use questions to guide conversations as you might use reins to gently guide a horse. With genuine inquiry, you can gracefully lead conversations toward an increase of harmony and intimacy. That's why learning how to use questions effectively is so essential. Questions hand you the reins and keep you leading, with love and wisdom, rather than following.

When you utilize this ability to guide conversations, you need not follow others into places you don't want to travel, including into conflicts that will worsen and strain the relationship. You can exercise your freedom to choose, with intention and forethought, how you want to conduct your communications, rather than allowing others to choose for you. You always possess the ability to blaze new trails toward extraordinary relationships by asking questions.

When someone confronts you with a statement, judgment, complaint, or criticism, resist the temptation to defend yourself or aggress in response. Opt to take a different path. Imagine that someone recommends that you walk off a cliff together. Do you have to? Of course not. You can choose to remain on solid ground and invite the other person to do the same with a question: "How about we just hang out here for a while instead?"

When you follow, you miss an opportunity to lead. When others confront you, you need not follow them into conflict. Let's look at this in action, starting with an example of a missed opportunity to lead and create a helpful conversation:

"You never want to have sex with me. What's your problem?"

"I'm tired when I get home and still have work to get done, and then I have to wake up before you do in the morning. I can only do so much!"

"You always make time to watch television. I don't see why you have time to watch TV but don't have time for me."

"That's different. I watch one show. It helps me unwind and takes my mind off things."

"And sex with me doesn't?"

"I'm exhausted. Can't I just be allowed to relax every once in a while? Nothing's ever good enough for you."

This dialogue demonstrates another key point about questions: Just because someone asks you a question doesn't mean you're obligated to answer it—especially if it isn't a genuine question. You can choose to guide instead, redirecting away from a counterproductive question by asking a thoughtful question of your own. Let's see how that might play out:

"You never want to have sex with me. What's your problem?"

"You think I never want to have sex with you?" (*This response recognizes that the question was actually more of a statement, something like "I want us to have sex" or "I want you to want to have sex with me." The response—a genuine question—gives permission and seeks to learn more. This is guiding.*)

"That's what it seems like."

"What makes you think that?" (*With this question, the second person doesn't disagree or get defensive. This question also doesn't offer any assurances that the second person actually does want to have sex. Instead, it shifts the dynamic so that the first person, who initiated the conversation from an emotionally reactive space, is now being guided.)*

"Because it's been over a month since the last time we had sex."

"And you would like us to be having sex more often?" *(This question steers the conversation toward a discussion about what the first person wants. This is the turning point of the conversation, showing that the second person cares about the first person's desires. The conversation is moving away from a problem and toward a solution.)*

"Definitely."

"Yeah, me too." *(Now the second person can articulate and embrace what both want, emphasizing that they aren't actually in opposition but want the same thing, that they are a team, facing and overcoming the same challenges together. An argument has been averted by taking a genuine interest in an opinion rather than fighting against it. Just one question guided a potential debate into a constructive conversation. This is the power of choosing inquiry.)*

The next time someone confronts you from an emotionally reactive state, experiment with taking an inquisitive stance. Instead of trying to prove a point, exercise curiosity and guide the interaction in a skillful way. The following guidelines may help:

1. Reorient someone who is acting out by asking questions aimed at discovering more about the person.

2. Remain calm, listen, and keep asking more questions, demonstrating that you aren't actually in opposition, but a team.

3. Guide the conversation toward a discussion of what the person wants.

4. Join the person in pursuit of solutions.

When you guide in this way, you'll see how it benefits your interactions. Over time, as you experiment, you'll learn what types of questions work best to cool heated moments and build extraordinary relationships. With practice, you can learn to redirect just about any confrontation toward healthy conversation.

67.

"FAMILIARITY FOSTERS FRIENDSHIP."

Your best friends are those you know extremely well. They understand you, and you understand them. Because you are familiar with one another, you each understand why the other thinks, feels, speaks, and acts in various ways. As such, you are quite permissive toward one another. For instance, when my best friend doesn't return my calls, I don't take it personally. Why? Because I know that's the way he is, and I give him permission for this because I value his friendship.

Often, the only thing keeping you from being friends with certain people is your lack of familiarity. If you knew one another better, perhaps having known each other since kindergarten, you would probably have developed a particular fondness for each other. You'd be friends because familiarity fosters friendship.

Whenever you want to cultivate an extraordinary relationship with someone, focus on increasing your familiarity with that person. Conversely, if you don't like someone, it's probably because you don't know that person, at least not well. You can remedy this by casting aside your judgments and seeking to learn more about the person. As your familiarity grows, the relationship will follow.

One of my favorite passages from *The Art of War*, by Sun Tzu, a general and philosopher in ancient China, underscores how crucial familiarity with oneself and others is in determining outcomes. He explains that the warrior who knows both the enemy and himself is never at risk, that the warrior who knows only himself and not the enemy may win or lose, and that the warrior who knows neither himself nor the enemy will always lose.

Since we aren't at war and others are not the enemy, let's translate this into terms more relevant to relationships and communication. Basically, the person who knows both another person and himself will never be at risk of an argument. The person who doesn't know the other person but knows himself will sometimes converse calmly and sometimes argue. And the person who knows neither the other person nor himself will be at risk of an argument in every interaction.

The goal is to know yourself and others well. Such familiarity greatly diminishes the potential for conflict. This is the point of asking questions: to increase familiarity. Let others share with you, and in turn, when asked, share with them. Exchange information—true information about what both of you think and feel. As you do so, familiarity grows. With this increased familiarity comes increased intimacy. You discover each other, and with this discovery, the relationship deepens.

If you notice that you aren't getting along with a certain person, then one of two things is true: either you don't know yourself well, or you don't know the other person well. As such, there's no need to argue. You can focus instead on remedying the true problem—your level of familiarity—through conversation.

Of course, you probably have a long history of making familiarity a priority in your relationships. You have probably tried, countless times, to get others to better understand you. If you've explained yourself over and over again, why isn't this working? There's a catch: You don't foster familiarity by trying to be understood. You foster familiarity by understanding.

68.

"UNDERSTANDING IS MORE IMPORTANT THAN BEING UNDERSTOOD."

No matter how hard you try, you can't guarantee that others will understand you. You can talk yourself blue in the face, explain yourself in a thousand ways, and still not ensure that another person understands you. What you can guarantee, however, is how well you understand others. If you ask thoughtful questions born from curiosity and truly listen to the responses, you can always increase your understanding of others.

Seeking to understand rather than be understood naturally relies more heavily on questions than statements. The process of inquiry is the path to discovery. This demonstrates your interest in the thoughts and feelings of others without judging or invalidating them. Conversation motivated by genuine curiosity also allows you to remain calm and nurture the relationship. Focus on how you treat others rather than on how they treat you. Focus on how you speak to others rather than on how they speak to you. Give permission and take responsibility. Along the way, familiarity will grow because you've made understanding your priority.

Whether others understand you isn't important. It's healthy to give permission for others to misunderstand. Meanwhile, the more you understand, the less you'll take things personally, and therefore the less you'll suffer. The less you suffer, the less suffering there will be in the relationship. In this way, developing understanding through calm and curious inquiry demonstrates compassion toward yourself, others, and your relationships.

69.
PRINCIPLE 5:
COOPERATIVENESS

The goal of communication is to promote conversations that inspire growth and change without harming relationships in the process. When two people argue, they are in opposition, as if sitting across a table from one another, each with their own perspective of some "problem" that rests between them.

Whenever you notice yourself in an argument with someone, understand that this is simply the dynamic that exists in the moment, and easily changed. If you metaphorically stand up, move to the other side of the table, and sit right next to this person, the two of you will no longer have combating perspectives; you'll share a common one. Once you're sitting together, you can view the issue from a common vantage point. This is cooperativeness.

When you take responsibility for your communications through cooperativeness, you join others on their side of the table. You do this because you understand that they want the same things you do. They want to be happy and get along. Because you care about them, you show them that you are a member of their team—that you are willing to listen to them, help them out, and cooperate. It's like saying, "Here, scoot over. Let's see how we can fix this thing together." Together, you can combine your resources, collaborate, and better achieve your common goals. As the adage goes, "Many hands make light work." Cooperativeness embraces this principle.

70.

"COOPERATIVE COMMUNICATION HAS AN ACHIEVABLE GOAL."

Conversations stall when achievable goals haven't been clearly defined. It's like playing a game where no one knows what the objective is. When would the game end? Only when it became tiresome. Indeed, bringing a conversation to successful completion requires that both participants understand the purpose for having the conversation.

Imagine that something happens and you react emotionally. You don't like the way you feel and assume that talking about it will make you feel better. Your momentum is pulling you out of your comfort zone and into confronting someone who is the presumed cause of your distress. When this happens, conflict usually follows. Why? Because your goal for communicating is to feel better. Unfortunately, this isn't a healthy goal for communication.

If you want to feel better, great! That's a fine motivation, but the means by which you accomplish this isn't through communication, but through giving permission. In reality, you have the ability to foster your own happiness. If your goal in communication is to vent, you can air your complaint. But out of compassion for others, you might want to let them know that this is your only goal. Let them know that your emotion has nothing to do with them, and that it isn't their responsibility to make you feel better. This way, you've stated your goal and made it achievable. This is highly cooperative.

When experiencing an emotional reaction, most people tend to confront others in an accusatory way. When this happens, they haven't clearly defined their goal; they just know how they feel and want the feeling changed somehow. As a result, they may judge or criticize, often leading others to become defensive or retaliate with judgments or criticisms of their own. The loop of doom commences, and the relationship is damaged unnecessarily. Such interactions can be avoided if you take a moment to articulate an achievable goal for the conversation.

You can simplify communication tremendously by announcing your intention for a conversation right at the outset, rather than holding the other person in suspense, and sometimes bafflement. You can use phrases like "I want you to know..." or "I want to know how you feel about...," rather than leaving others guessing. This supports cooperativeness by making it easier for others to understand what you want to achieve.

If your goal is to tell your partner how you feel, that's achievable. If your goal is to discover how your partner feels, you can accomplish that through inquiry. When you set a goal for communication, make sure it's achievable. Here are some examples of achievable goals: "I want to communicate that I'm frustrated he never does the dishes," "I want to find out whether she has ever thought about getting a divorce," or "I want to tell him how much I enjoyed the card he wrote me." These goals are achievable because they are defined by actions that are your choice, your own expression.

Goals that are defined by the actions of others aren't always achievable, since you can't control others. Here are some examples of goals that aren't under your control: "I want him to start doing the dishes," "I want her to tell me that she has never thought about divorce," or "I want him to feel appreciated by me." These goals may be achieved through communication, but you can't guarantee that they will be.

By setting achievable goals, you can create productive conversations that are cooperative in nature. When communications falter, pause for a moment to identify your purpose and help others identify theirs so communication can become purposeful again. When communication is purposeful, it flows.

71.
"WHAT DOES THE OTHER PERSON WANT YOU TO KNOW?"

Imagine getting caught in an argument with your partner that's going in circles. You're starting to feel frustrated and want the communication to take a productive turn. Noticing this, you can choose to guide the conversation toward the articulation of specific goals, and you can do so in a completely cooperative way.

For example, you might start by saying, "Can I ask you a question?" This invites your partner to listen. Remember, questions open doors. A question like this is analogous to knocking gently on your partner's door. If she wants to hear what you have to say, she'll open the door and invite your communication inward. She's listening.

Then you might ask, "What is it that you want me to know right now?" This is a magnificent question. It gives your partner the opportunity to stop to think about her own goal for the communication. At the same time, it shows her that you're interested in what she has to say, that you're cooperating with her, and that there is therefore no need to keep fighting. This allows her to slow down enough to sense that you want to see and hear her. Here's an example of how the conversation might proceed:

"I want you to know that I'm pissed you didn't call to tell me you were going to come home so late. I was worried sick about you." (*This is probably a reiteration of something that's already been said.*)

"You wanted me to call you to tell you I'd be late?" (*This confirms the goal.*)

"Of course! All you ever think about is yourself!"

"And because I didn't call, you were worried about me?" (*Rather than getting distracted by your partner's somewhat aggressive characterization of you, give permission, remain nondefensive, and focus on creating a solution. Instead of following, keep guiding.*)

"I was, a lot."

"And you don't want to worry about me?" (*This brings the discussion to the topic of what your partner wants.*)

"Of course not. I didn't get a wink of sleep."

"Well, I don't want you to worry about me either. In the future, I'll make an effort to call when I know I'm going to be late. Would that help?" (*The future is more important than the past, since the past can't be changed. Therefore, it's helpful to redirect attention away from what can't be changed toward that which can be: the future.*)

"It would."

"Okay, that makes sense. I'm willing to make an effort to do that." (*This response doesn't offer any promises, but it does set the intention and confirms that your partner's goal for the communication has been achieved.*)

"Thanks."

This is how you can transform an argument into a constructive conversation. Ask questions that articulate goals, then respond to this information with follow-up questions aimed at understanding. Sidestep each opportunity for conflict and focus on solutions. Don't challenge complaints or criticisms or fight to defend yourself or change the person's mind. Rather, show compassion, stay open and receptive, and seek to learn more. When you do this, you show others that you care about improving your relationship with them. You work with them rather than against them. This is cooperation.

72.

"ASK THE OTHER PERSON TO HELP YOU UNDERSTAND."

Whenever someone makes a comment to you, even (perhaps especially) one you dislike, view it as a reflection of who that person is in the moment. Take it as an opportunity to learn more. After all, your lack of understanding is what makes it difficult to give permission—and therefore what makes the comment seem unpleasant.

Imagine your partner tells you, "I'm tired of you complaining about every little thing I do." If you fight against such a remark, it won't take long to enter the loop of doom. So instead, try to understand why he thinks and feels this way with a question such as "Help me understand why you think I complain about everything you do."

Saying, "Help me understand," is an extremely effective communication tool—and one that probably goes a bit against your training. Let's face it, like most people, you've probably been trained how to argue, assert your viewpoint, and prove yourself right and others wrong. You've been trained to compete. But this isn't cooperative, and it doesn't benefit your relationships.

Beginning a statement with "Help me understand..." can quickly transform an adversarial moment into a cooperative one. You ask for help with understanding. This is probably what others want anyway: for you to understand something about them. As such, you unify your goals with theirs. If you share a single goal for the conversation, with a little teamwork it can probably be accomplished.

73.

"YOU HEAD IN THE DIRECTION YOU FACE."

I once took a motorcycle driving course, where I learned that, when navigating a turn, it's best to fix your eyes upon the exit of the turn. Why? Because the motorcycle naturally follows your gaze. Likewise, when we point the nose of a boat in a certain direction, this is the direction the boat travels, and when we point an arrow in a certain direction and release the bowstring, this is the direction the arrow flies. The same is true in relationships. Where we aim our attention matters.

The thought *I'm so mad at my partner I could scream!* keeps you feeling angry. *My job sucks* keeps your experience at work unsatisfactory. *No one loves me* keeps you feeling unloved. Fixing your gaze on what you don't want moves you farther in that direction.

So much energy is squandered when we focus on problems rather than solutions. Since solutions are the goal, this is the more productive direction to face. Instead of trying to fix things that are "wrong," activate your imagination and strive to build what you want. Aim to be creative rather than corrective, and join others in a shared journey of this kind of creativity. If you are seeking extraordinary relationships, this is where to fix your gaze. If you do this, you'll inevitably travel in the direction of solutions, and you'll bring others along with you.

74.
"THERE ARE NO SOLUTIONS IN THE PAST."

It is truly astounding how often people find themselves arguing about the past. Someone thinks, feels, says, or does something that another person doesn't like, and then an argument ensues. Unfortunately, no amount of dispute can change events that have already transpired. As such, arguing about the past is a complete misuse of time and energy. There are no solutions in the past. In the present and future, however, solutions abound.

Imagine your partner tells you that something you did was mean. He's focusing on the past. If you respond by saying, "No it wasn't," you are not only invalidating his opinion, but also needlessly focusing your attention where it isn't very useful. Why focus on what you cannot change rather than what you can? It's more effective to focus on the present and future.

In this case, the present is how your partner is currently judging the past, how he is, in this moment, looking back on some action of yours and evaluating it as "mean." Why not give him permission to think this way, then shift your focus (and his) from what has already happened to what's happening now.

To reorient attention from the past to the present—what the person is currently thinking—ask something like "You think what I did was mean?" Instead of addressing the past action, address the present judgment. Commit to discovery, rather than judgment or defense, and ask something like "What makes you think so?" When your partner responds, you'll learn more about him and better understand why he feels this way.

Rather than trying to convince your partner that he's wrong, that you aren't mean, you can demonstrate this in the present moment by relating to him in a caring and attentive way. To this end, you might say, "Okay, I understand now why you thought that was mean of me. In the future, what do you want me to do in that situation instead?" This exhibits cooperativeness by focusing on the future, where solutions are infinite.

Using solution-focused questions is paramount for skillful communication. You can always change the direction of any argument, no matter how heated, by reorienting from problems to solutions. Here are some suggestions:

- "In the future, how would you like me to handle something like this?"

- "Next time, what would you want me to say instead?"

- "Can you think of a way we can avoid this happening again?"

Share the opportunity for creating solutions by approaching others in a spirit of cooperation and soliciting ideas about possible solutions. Rather than trying to guess what someone wants, ask. This allows you to continue building an extraordinary relationship. The next time you find yourself in an argument, try this:

1. Listen to what you're arguing about. Chances are, you're arguing about the past.

2. Address the *present* by asking this person about what she is thinking and feeling right now. Help the other person focus on her current thoughts or feelings about the past, rather than the past itself.

3. Address the *future* by asking this person what she wants moving forward. Instead of trying to correct the past, focus on what you both want in common, and work together to create this. Now, that's cooperation. Well done!

75.

REFLECTION POINT: RESPONSIBILITY FOR YOUR COMMUNICATIONS

Before moving to part 6, Taking Responsibility for Your Choices, let's review the five "iconic" principles of responsible communication: I implement...

- **Calm:** Operate from within your emotional comfort zone by giving permission. When you communicate, make remaining calm your top priority.

- **Objectivity:** Speak and think in language that is "inarguably true." Rely on statements that are undeniable, communicating truthfully and factually, remembering the power of "maybe," and shifting focus from "need" or "should" to "want." This helps avoid disagreements.

- **Neutrality:** Be neither aggressive nor defensive. Avoid attacking others with complaints, criticisms, or character assessments. Recognize that there's no need to defend yourself; you aren't being attacked—others are simply revealing themselves to you.

- **Inquiry:** Ask questions in the spirit of curiosity, aiming for understanding rather than being understood. Ask questions in an effort to increase familiarity and guide communication toward solutions.

- **Cooperativeness:** Work together toward achieving common goals, joining others in a spirit of teamwork. Show others you aren't their adversary, but their ally, by employing all five principles of responsible communication.

PART 6

TAKING
RESPONSIBILITY FOR
YOUR CHOICES

76.
"CHOICE IS FREEDOM."

Choice is freedom. Embrace this freedom—both your own right to choose and that of others. Make everything about choices, and nothing about obligations. Obviously, no one is obligated to be how you want them to be, nor are you obligated to be the way others want. You get to choose for yourself, as does everyone else. Realizing this, you can take responsibility for your own quality of life by taking responsibility for your choices.

Most people don't realize how much freedom they have. Indeed, you may feel yoked by the expectations and judgments of others, as well as by the expectations and judgments you have of yourself. After all, you don't want to disappoint, upset, or sadden anyone. You probably want others to admire, respect, and like you. That's normal, but as long as you have this orientation, your life will be somewhat encumbered by a sense of obligation to be what others want you to be.

Living a life of obligation comes with a cost. When we act out of a sense of obligation, we do so unwillingly and we inevitably harbor resentment toward ourselves or others because we feel forced to do something not of our choosing. We may even aggress against this. We may grumble, gripe, groan, and bellyache about these perceived obligations. If so, we're acting out. This doesn't help us or our relationships. Yet, ironically, we feel obligated because we want to help. The intent is sound, but the approach is flawed.

Imagine that your partner invites you to go out together but you're tired and would rather stay home. You suspect she'll get angry if you don't go, so you immediately feel trapped in a no-win situation. If you go out, you're likely to make an issue about it, wanting her to know that you're doing this against your will. You'll want your sacrifice to be recognized. In some way, your actions or attitude will convey, *See? Don't say I never do things for you* or *See? I obviously care about you because I am doing this even though I don't want to.*

Instead, why not tell your partner, "No, thanks. I'm tired and I'm choosing to stay home tonight." What then? Yes, she may get angry. You could add, "Since I'm tired, I won't be fun to be with and that could ruin your experience. So rather than doing something that wouldn't be kind to either of us, I'd rather respect our relationship and take a rain check." If she wants to go out, she can still go without you. She gets to do what she wants, just like you. This isn't as selfish as it may seem. When you exercise your freedom to choose, everyone benefits. You extend kindness toward yourself, and as a result, your relationships will prosper all the more in the long run.

It's the big picture that matters, not just each vignette along the way. Going out when you don't want to, out of a sense of obligation, would be focusing only on the small picture. While you may seem to be keeping the peace in the moment, you would be reinforcing codependency and limiting the potential for health and growth in your relationship. Which is more important: going out this one particular evening or creating an extraordinary relationship? Of course, creating a truly healthy relationship is your greater goal, so, if you don't want to go out, don't go—not because you're selfish, but because you want to cultivate an extraordinary relationship, a relationship that respects and supports the freedom of both people, and what both want, equally.

Taking responsibility for your choices means recognizing that no one is ever truly obligated to do anything. Embrace choices that promote your happiness, and support others in making similar choices for themselves.

77.
"YOU CAN CHOOSE SOLUTIONS."

Whenever you react emotionally, whenever you suffer, there are always choices available to you. You have a right to alleviate your suffering by choosing solutions. What you don't have is the right to expect others to alleviate your suffering. Give others their freedom and embrace your own.

Imagine that you're sitting beside your partner watching television together and he starts loudly munching on potato chips. Distracted by this, you feel annoyed. Maybe you try to give permission, hoping he'll stop soon, yet you find yourself increasingly irritated. If you suppress your irritation, you aren't taking responsibility for finding a solution. After all, you aren't expected or required to enjoy everything you encounter in life, and that's not what giving permission is about. Because your irritation comes from within you, you can make choices that will remedy your discomfort.

Recognizing this, you could bark, "Stop that! You're driving me bonkers!" In fact, acting out this way might produce the result you want, but it will also injure the relationship, even if only slightly. A more constructive choice might be to change your posture or move to another chair. Or you might choose to communicate about this directly, without negative tone or judgment: "I'm having difficulty focusing on the show while you're eating." With this statement, you're only sharing information. In all likelihood, this information will inspire change. If your partner stops or eats more quietly, then great, mission accomplished. If not, that's his right, and that's fine too. You can continue to exercise your right to choose a solution. You could turn up the volume a notch or joke around playfully about what's going on. It matters less what choice you make than that you make one, and that you do so in a nonjudging and nonblaming way. This is more than a freedom, it's a responsibility—at least if you want to cultivate extraordinary relationships.

Taking responsibility for your choices also works retroactively. Here's an example: I purchased a cup of coffee from a drive-through, then I got back on the road, only to have the cup tilt out of my cup holder, spilling coffee in my lap. Before I could think, I was seriously perturbed. I was pissed at the coffee shop for serving the coffee so hot, pissed at the cup for not having a better lid, and pissed at the auto manufacturer for not designing a better cup holder. There had to be someone to blame—someone or something besides myself. Then it dawned on me that I could have done something, many things in fact, to avoid this incident. After all, it wasn't news to me that I had a lousy cup holder. I could have chosen to secure the cup with my hand while turning, as I had many times before. I could have turned onto the road more slowly. I could have implemented a variety of solutions. Once I took responsibility for the fact that I didn't make a choice I could have made, my anger vanished and I started to playfully laugh at myself.

The responsibility for negative emotions is never external. Once we recognize that we are responsible for our emotions, we empower ourselves to be the solution. And while the past doesn't offer solutions, it does allow us to learn from our experiences and make different choices in the future. I'm glad to be able to report that although I continue to frequent that same coffee shop, never again have I spilled my coffee when turning out onto the road.

78.
"EVERYONE GETS TO DO WHAT THEY WANT."

You may think that if everyone were to do whatever they want, the result would be anarchy. The truth is, if everyone did exactly what they wanted—what they truly wanted, rather than what they may think they want—that would be a paradise in which everyone thrived emotionally and got along well with one another. On a deep level, everyone wants to experience a sense of personal fulfill‑ ment and have rich, rewarding relationships. And everyone wants this for others no less than they want it for themselves. If everyone lived in accordance with these deepest desires, the result would be bliss.

Not only do you get to do what you want, you actually owe this to yourself and to others. You can live your ideal life and be your ideal self. You can be whoever and however you choose. The truer you are to yourself, the happier you'll be. It's a choice to respect yourself and support what you do and don't want. If you don't do this for yourself, who will?

Perhaps this sounds too selfish, catering to your own desires all the time. Well, guess what? If that's not what you want, then you don't have to. Why? Because you get to do what you want!

Besides, doing what you want is selfish only when viewed super‑ ficially. When you look deeper, you can discover the selflessness in it. When you do what you want or don't do what you don't want, you build a loving relationship with yourself. You become a person who truly supports you, a person who gives you permission to be who you are. In this way, you build an extraordinary relationship with yourself.

You can always consider what others want, as well. If you want to hug your partner because you know she enjoys being hugged, that's fine; you can do it. Just acknowledge exactly why you're doing it: because you want to, plain and simple—because it's your choice. This choice is informed by your familiarity with your partner; in this case, your knowledge that she enjoys hugs. If this makes you want to hug her, great! You get to do what you want. The important thing to grasp here is that you do whatever you do because it's what you want to do. By taking responsibility for your choices in this way, you'll live more authentically. When you live more authentically, you'll live more joyfully.

Perhaps you're thinking something along the lines of "Hey, we all have to do things we don't want to do sometimes. That's just life." Actually, that isn't life; it's only how life appears to be. If you don't want to hug your partner, you don't have to. If you don't want to go to work, you can stay home. If you want to smoke weed all day and watch *Three's Company* reruns, you can do just that. This is your life, and you get to conduct it as you please.

Sure, there will be consequences. If you don't hug your partner, she may feel unloved and start to drift away. If you don't go to work, you might get fired. If you smoke weed all day while watching *Three's Company* reruns, you probably won't accomplish other things that may be more meaningful to you in the meantime. Regardless, you're still allowed to drift apart from your partner if you want, get fired if you want, or not be ambitious if you want. You're free to choose for yourself.

But you're no fool. You know your choices have consequences, and you usually take this into account. When you hug your partner even though you don't necessarily feel like it, you do so because you don't want her to feel unloved; therefore, you want to hug her. When you go to work when you'd rather not, you do so because you don't want to get fired; therefore, you want to go to work. When you stay home all day smoking weed and watching *Three's Company* reruns even as you tell yourself you should be doing more with your life, you do so because that's one hilarious show and you just can't get enough of it; in other words, because you want to.

Recognize that the life you live is one of choice—your choice. If you don't like a given choice, you can choose something different. When you fail to do what you want to do or you choose to do what you don't want to do, you pay a price. The price is resentment. If you go out with your partner when you don't feel like it, you'll probably harbor some resentment. You may even spend some or all of your time then letting her know just how unhappy you are in a passive-aggressive way. In essence, that's punishing someone for a choice that you yourself made. Your partner didn't make the choice for you to go out, no matter how much guilt-tripping or cajoling she might have done.

By being true to yourself, you foster your own joyfulness and spare others any resentment you might have held for feeling like you were forced into something you didn't want to do. This is why you do what you want and don't do what you don't want: because acting out of a sense of obligation invites resentment into the relationship. Trying to be selfless and putting your own wants aside in favor of what others want just doesn't work.

When you recognize that you have a right to do what you want, you take responsibility for your choices. When you recognize that others have the same right, you can be truly supportive in your relationships. You give permission for others to choose to do what they want and not do what they don't want. This freedom is paramount for extraordinary relationships. Therefore, when building extraordinary relationships, what both people want is the most important, and hopefully most frequent, topic of conversation.

79.

"CHOICE IS ABOUT UNDERSTANDING WHAT YOU WANT."

Your desires are one of the purest reflections of who you are at any moment. You go to an ice cream store and want chocolate or vanilla or strawberry. Why? It doesn't matter. You just want that flavor, and the reasons are completely irrelevant. You're allowed to want what you want, and others are allowed to want what they want. Give them this permission.

In taking responsibility for your choices, it's important to understand what you want, and what others want, as well. Some of the most meaningful communication you can have with your partner is about what each of you wants. When you communicate your desires, you're sharing information. When you inquire about desires, you're soliciting valuable information that may in turn influence what you want.

Communicating what you want takes a measure of assertiveness. To express your desires, to put them out into the conversation, it's important to know that they have value—to know that you deserve to be happy, safe, and loved, and that you deserve to have your wishes met, at least some of the time, for a natural reciprocity to occur. When you communicate what you want to others without implying any obligation that they provide you with what you want, this is an act of generosity. After all, if others don't know what you want, they can't make informed choices about what they themselves want to do or don't want to do based on this information. With this approach, you share information about yourself in a factual, no-strings-attached way that remains objective. What others choose to do with this information is entirely up to them. You're just being generous and sharing information.

When you inquire about what someone else wants, ideally you do so because you genuinely want to know. You're curious. Why? Because knowing what others want shapes what you yourself want; it educates you and helps you make choices about what you want to do. Returning to the example of going out, before proclaiming you don't want to go and are therefore choosing to stay home, you might first ask a question so your decision will be better informed. For instance, you might ask, "How badly do you want me to be there with you?" If your partner says, "It would mean the world to me," this information might change what it is you want to do. Now you may find yourself genuinely *wanting* to go, not out of obligation, but out of choice.

Because knowing what both parties want is so essential to cultivating extraordinary relationships, here are some tips:

- **To value your own desires:**
  - Communicate what you want to others, understanding that they have no obligation to provide it to you.
  - Respect the freedom of others to choose for themselves what to do with the information that you've shared with them. Give them this permission.

- **To value the desires of others:**
  - Inquire about what they want, understanding you have no obligation whatsoever to provide it to them.
  - Respect your freedom to choose for yourself what to do with the information that has been shared with you. Give yourself this permission.

80.
"CHOICE CONSIDERS WILLINGNESS."

In relationships, we often want our partners to do various things. You might want your partner to remember to lock the front door each night or be nicer to you. However, insisting on these things would probably lead to resistance and therefore be less than effective. What can you do instead? You can inquire about your partner's willingness.

My wife has become a master at this. For example, she might ask, "Are you willing to do the dishes tonight?" or "Are you willing to come with me to visit my parents this weekend?" In this way, she simply solicits information. Nine times out of ten, my answer is "Sure!" Why? Because she has respected my freedom to choose for myself. I understand that her question expresses something she wants, and that if I am genuinely willing, I can take this opportunity to provide it of my own free will. This approach supports my freedom to choose.

Knowing what you are willing and unwilling to do will help you take responsibility for your choices. Knowing what others are willing and unwilling to do will help you better understand them and give permission. If someone is unwilling to do something, give permission for this. You might ask more about the reasons for the unwillingness. This opens the door to a conversation in which you will discover more about one another, and the relationship will naturally flow more smoothly in the future.

81.
"GETTING WHAT YOU WANT IS YOUR CHOICE."

Even if you convey what you want to others, you may not get it. Is it because they don't care about your wishes? Perhaps, but more often it's because others are unable to give what you're asking. They may want to but, for whatever reason, cannot. So how can you increase the likelihood of getting what you want?

Let's say you want twenty dollars from someone because you think you can't be happy without it. You ask this person for twenty dollars and he gives you ten. Every time you again ask for twenty, he gives only ten. Over time, you probably start to feel insulted or hurt. You may even get furious at him: "How rude! Weren't you listening to me? How can I be happy with ten bucks?"

If you react this way, you aren't giving permission. What if this person only has ten dollars to give? What if he's giving you 100 percent of what he has and can't give a penny more? No amount of ranting and raving is going to increase the amount he has to offer. Perhaps he's being as generous as he can possibly be. If you knew this, you wouldn't see any reason to complain or get upset. You'd gratefully accept what was given.

In relationships, you might ask your partner for more of something—more love, affection, respect, or whatever—and then get frustrated when he offers you less than you desire. You assume he's able to give more than he is, that he's withholding and deliberately not giving all he can.

The truth is, everyone is always giving 100 percent of what they have to give at any moment. Perhaps your partner once gave you what you're asking for now. If so, it's because, back then, he had it to give. That he gives less now simply reveals that this is the most he can give at this time. Actually, less has changed than it may seem. He's still giving 100 percent. If you don't understand this, you might get resentful. You might fruitlessly petition him to give you more and then feel neglected when he doesn't. Fortunately, when you want more from someone than what he has to give, you have some healthier options—three, to be precise.

Option one. You can understand that what has changed is not your partner, but the relationship, and then try to figure out how the relationship has changed. If you explore this, you might find that there are factors that have diminished your partner's ability to give what he once gave. You can identify any obstacles and work together to remove them. This will probably allow your partner's 100 percent to expand. You may get what you want not by insisting, but by collaborating with your partner to improve the relationship.

For example, imagine that you want more affection from your partner. Instead of fighting for this, you choose to converse about it and ask him, with genuine curiosity, why he's no longer as affectionate with you. Perhaps he tells you that he can't bear the smell of cigarettes on you. That's news to you, and when you think about it, you realize that his affection waned around the same time you started smoking again. This makes sense, and you see that if you want more affection, you can do something about it: you can quit smoking. By focusing on solutions (in this case, quitting smoking), you may find that your partner again has more to give.

Option two. When you don't get as much as you want, you can appreciate what you are given and see it as sufficient. When you do this, you embrace your partner's limitations. You give permission for your partner to give whatever he has to give in the moment. This can accomplish wonders. When you embrace what others have to give and are sincerely grateful for it, the amount they're able to give tends to grow. Giving others permission to be who and how they are is nourishing. Being accepted fully is an utterly joyful experience, and that joy makes it possible for others to have more to share with you.

Remember the married couple who eventually decided to live separately? Before they came to this solution, the husband had spent many months complaining that he wasn't getting enough affection, yet his wife began offering him even less. When he started giving permission instead, the amount of affection his wife was able to willingly give increased.

Option three. It's possible that your partner is incapable of giving more, and that no amount of conversation, asking for what you want, understanding, cooperation, or giving permission is going to change that. Perhaps he will forever have certain limitations on what he can give because that's how he was raised. And perhaps you know that, as long as you live, you'll continue to want more. In this case, it's best to stop fighting for what you can't get. You and your partner will both be happier if you agree to part ways. You may find someone who can give you what you want, and your partner may find someone who will be sincerely content receiving what he's capable of offering. Parting ways can be the best option for both people. In the end, both will be happier.

82.
"YOU CAN ADD WHAT'S MISSING."

If you know you want to see more of something in one of your relationships, you can add more of it, whatever it may be, yourself. You can add what's missing. Remember, you can't choose for others. You can only choose for yourself. Adding what you think is missing is another way to take responsibility for your choices.

It's as if you're making a soup with your partner, let's say minestrone. You each add various ingredients and share the responsibility of stirring it occasionally, tending to it with care. Suddenly, you decide that there aren't enough tomatoes in the soup. Because you view minestrone as a tomato soup, this is a pretty important oversight. You exclaim to your partner, "We need more tomatoes! Quick, throw them in!" She disagrees: "Nah, it's fine the way it is." But you know how you like your minestrone and that it would be tastier with more tomatoes in it. "Seriously! We don't have enough tomatoes yet. Put more in or it's going to taste awful. Trust me on this." Maybe your partner continues to disagree, or maybe she agrees but simply doesn't have any tomatoes to add or doesn't know where to find them. However, you know exactly where they are. They're in your hands! If you continue to insist with ever-increasing intensity that your partner add the tomatoes to the soup, they'll never be added. And on top of that, your joint cooking experience will be spoiled by this unnecessary conflict. Either your partner will storm out of the kitchen in frustration or you will. The solution is obvious: put in the tomatoes yourself.

A relationship is like this minestrone. You're allowed to strive for what you think will be delicious. You can do this on your own, guided by your own tastes and preferences. You don't need anyone else's permission to create the relationship you desire, nor do you need anyone else's cooperation. If your partner thinks the relationship that you create is too bland, spicy, or bitter, or if she simply doesn't want what you have made, this is something you can discuss together. Perhaps you can agree upon a new recipe. If not, perhaps your tastes are simply too different to reconcile.

You owe it to yourself to prepare something you'll savor. Creating the relationship you desire is up to you and you alone. This is a healthy way to view your relationships. The important thing to understand is that it doesn't make sense to demand that others create the relationship you want to have with them—not when you can create it on your own by adding whatever you think is missing. This is the power you exercise when you take responsibility for your choices. If you want more hugs, hug more. If you want more respect, show more respect. If you want to be appreciated, show gratitude. When you see something missing, add this absent ingredient. By giving permission and taking responsibility, you can create extraordinary and richly satisfying relationships.

83.
"RESPECT THE MIDDLE LINE."

Imagine a circle divided by a line down the middle. Now imagine that this circle is the space within which a relationship occurs. You stand in one half, and your partner stands in the other. You can roam wherever you choose within your space, and your partner can roam wherever he chooses within his.

In extraordinary relationships, both partners respect the middle line. If you want intimacy with your partner, you travel to the middle line and no farther. If he wants the same thing at that moment, you'll find him there. If not, give permission for this and wait until he arrives to join you.

If you're impatient for intimacy, you may be tempted to cross the line to go get your partner. This is a common mistake and shows that you don't give your partner permission to choose for himself. In essence, when you cross the middle line, you trespass. This may show up as complaints about not getting enough affection or, more passive-aggressively, as pouting or withdrawing. Although your goal may be intimacy, your partner is likely to respond by moving farther away, perhaps outside the circle altogether. After all, if your partner equally wanted intimacy at the same time you did, he would have been in the middle when you got there. Or if you had waited a moment, maybe he would have shown up as soon as he felt comfortable. One thing is for certain: trespassing pushes others away. If you trespass often enough, your partner may opt to move outside the circle altogether, ending the relationship.

The only thing that genuinely achieves intimacy is giving permission. It's like interacting with a stray dog. Most strays are leery of strangers, having been mistreated in the past. If you run toward such a dog, even if all you want to do is pet it, it's likely to flee. It will manage the emotional distance between itself and you and move to a place where it feels safe. If you stand still instead, maybe crouching and holding out a treat, little by little the dog will move nearer. If you respect the emotional distance the dog prefers and patiently wait in the middle, it will probably join you eventually, arriving when it feels at ease. Only then will it accept your love and affection. Or maybe it's unable to trust and will run away regardless. If so, that's okay. You can only do so much—and that includes not crossing the middle line. Although it may not work every time, it's the only thing that stands any chance of creating a loving and trusting relationship.

To cultivate extraordinary relationships, give permission for others to position themselves wherever they feel comfortable in relation to you. If you go to the middle line, wait for your partner, and find that he has no inclination to join you there no matter how long you wait, you have a choice. Standing at the middle, you can communicate in a calm and intentional way: "I'm here and I want you to join me. If you don't, that's okay. I want you to do what you want." If he's still unable to join you, recognize this as a reflection of his current ability. Continuing to give permission usually helps increase the other person's comfort level, so he may eventually approach. If not, you can choose to seek another relationship.

What if your partner crosses the middle line, trespassing and disregarding your comfort level? What then? Again, you have a choice. You can communicate what you want and see how your partner responds. If he's indifferent to your wishes and continues to trespass, you can choose to remove yourself from the circle. You deserve to be in an extraordinary relationship, a relationship in which both partners respect the middle line, and each other, willingly and completely.

84.
Reflection Point: Responsibility for Your Choices

Before moving on, let's review the fundamentals of taking responsibility for your choices:

- If you notice a "problem," embrace yourself as the solution. Consider what you can do differently and what choices you can make individually rather than focusing on what others can do differently.

- Understanding what you and others want is essential for making informed choices about your relationships. Remember, desires change over the course of any relationship, especially those that last multiple decades or through life transitions. Collecting information about one another's ever-changing wants is invaluable.

- You have the ability to get what you want, with or without another person's cooperation. You can nurture your relationships in a way that builds harmony and intimacy. As the relationship improves, you may find yourself getting what you always wanted without ever asking for it.

- Embrace your own individuality and wholeheartedly support the individuality of others. You have your choices to make, and others have theirs. This is what taking responsibility for your choices looks like: embracing your freedom and that of others and giving permission all the while. Freedom is the fuel of extraordinary relationships.

PART 7

THE END
AND THE
BEGINNING

85.
A Brief Overview

The two truths about love—the art of giving permission and the wisdom of taking responsibility—honor both people in a relationship equally. By combining and embracing these two skills, you can cultivate extraordinary relationships, not only with others, but with yourself and your life. Let's quickly review the basic principles of this philosophy so that you can better put these truths into action.

Most of all, remember that you have the ability to transform yourself and your relationships, all on your own, by making a commitment to alleviating your suffering, which arises from within. This suffering reveals itself in the form of emotional reactions to external events. As you now know, external events are never the true cause of suffering; your relationship to them is. Whenever you experience an emotional reaction, it's because you aren't giving permission.

Whenever you experience an emotional reaction, your emotion has moved outside of your comfort zone. Returning to your comfort zone will accomplish the two goals of giving permission: you'll feel better, and you'll maximize your ability to respond with intentionality. To do this, follow the five steps of giving permission:

1. Recognize that you're reacting

2. Pause

3. Breathe

4. Understand why it makes sense to give permission

5. Give permission

When you give permission, you're taking responsibility for your emotions. This lays the foundation for taking responsibility for both your communications and your choices. This trio of responsibilities creates the path to extraordinary relationships.

When you take responsibility for your emotions, you focus on yourself and your emotional autonomy. You understand that all of your emotions come from you, and you take responsibility for transforming your emotional reactions as they arise so you can be as effective as possible in promoting the growth of your relationships.

By taking responsibility for your emotions, you become better able to take responsibility for your communications. This is essential, because it is through constructive conversation that familiarity grows. Such conversation is governed by the five "iconic" principles: I implement...

- **Calm:** communicating from within the emotional comfort zone

- **Objectivity:** making statements that are "inarguably true"

- **Neutrality:** communicating in a way that is neither aggressive nor defensive

- **Inquiry:** asking questions in a spirit of genuine curiosity

- **Cooperativeness:** working with others toward common goals

Taking responsibility for your choices reminds you that you have the freedom—and the responsibility—to make your own decisions about how to live your life while respecting that the same is also true for others. You get to make your own choices; others get to make theirs.

Following, you'll find a visual summary of what the book has discussed up to this point. This is the heart of the philosophy behind *The Two Truths about Love*. In the remaining chapters, I'll address an assortment of topics that can support this philosophy in cultivating extraordinary relationships. These chapters comprise the end, but also the beginning...

EVENT

Emotional Reaction
(Physiological)

Not Giving Permission Judging, blaming, criticizing, controlling, punishing, freezing, fleeing, fighting	**Giving Permission** Recognize, pause, breathe, understand the ABCs, give permission
Acting Out Outside comfort zone Unintentional and reactive	**Acting In** Inside comfort zone Intentional and responsive
Making Others Responsible For your own emotions For your own communications and choices	**Taking Responsibility** For your own emotions For your own communications and choices
Codependency	**Emotional Autonomy**
Unhealthy Attachment Rigid, needy, fearful	**Healthy Attachment** Flexible, independent, fearless
Aiming for Control Expressing "needs" and "shoulds" Limiting freedom	**Aiming for Influence** Expressing wants Supporting freedom
Argument Holding on to competing goals Correcting "problems"	**Conversation** Seeking cooperative goals Creating solutions
Discord	**Harmony**
Distance	**Intimacy**
Ordinary Relationships	**Extraordinary Relationships**

86.
"SELF-CARE MATTERS."

Whether you're using your body to run a marathon or your mind to give a presentation at work, how well you perform depends in part upon your physical state in the moment. Even if you're a seasoned runner, you may find yourself unable to complete a race if you don't get sufficient sleep the night before. If you arrive at work with a hangover, you may lack the mental sharpness to articulate your ideas effectively. It's no different with the skills of giving permission and taking responsibility. If you want to excel at the tools in this book and create the life and relationships you desire, good self-care will always play a role.

The healthier you are physically, the more effortlessly you'll find you can give permission and take responsibility. As such, make your physical health a priority. Rest and eat well. Spare yourself the burden of harmful addictions, and find enjoyable ways to be active. Your physical wellness in a particular moment can significantly widen or narrow the size of your emotional comfort zone. Those who are physically healthy have a much larger emotional comfort zone than those who are not. Knowing this, respect the effect that your lifestyle has on your ability to cultivate extraordinary relationships and give yourself—and everyone you interact with—the compassionate gift of a healthy and vibrant you.

87.
"EMBRACE THE POWER OF 'OKAY.'"

"Okay" is my favorite word in the English language. Why? Because it epitomizes giving permission. "Okay" allows. It shrugs off anything and everything. It keeps us in our wisdom and strengthens our relationships. "Okay" cultivates harmony and intimacy like no other word can. I honestly think that if I had to choose only one word to use for the rest of my life, it would be "okay" (with "thanks" close behind in second place).

No matter what someone says to you, no matter how far it is from what you want to hear, you can always respond with "okay," even if you only do so silently to yourself. This will remind you that everyone has the right to think what they think, feel what they feel, say what they say, and do what they do. This isn't a right you give them, but a right they have inherently. If you don't let this be okay, then you'll only make yourself suffer and precipitate conflict. The more you can genuinely be okay with others, yourself, and the world in general, the more joyful your life will be and the more others will enjoy being around you.

"Okay" is amazingly disarming—the aikido master that gracefully redirects any and all aggression harmlessly to the wayside. It keeps you calm, centered, and free from injury:

"You're going to live to regret this."

"Okay."

It also serves as a reminder that there's no need to convince others of anything or insist that they see things as you do. Let others think what they think. After all, all opinions are true—as merely that: opinions. This also applies to self-talk:

"I hate the way I look."

"Okay."

"Okay" lets whatever is true be true and embraces it gladly. This one little word allows us to attend to anything and everything with gracefulness. Using it will enhance your ability to remain calm, think clearly, act intentionally, create constructive conversations, and move toward solutions. Everyone wants and deserves to be joyful, and saying "okay" can help us achieve this goal with supreme skillfulness and efficacy. To live a full and contented life, a life that is flexible in the face of stress and strain, consider invoking this word often—in its true spirit.

The true spirit of "okay" is one of wisdom and compassion. Use it because you understand that it is truly okay for people to think what they think, feel what they feel, say what they say, and do what they do, given that this is a reflection of who a person is at any given moment. This is wisdom. Use it because you also understand that being okay with who another person is allows you to transcend judgment and give permission—a profoundly generous act that promotes the healthy growth of relationships and benefits your own emotional wellness. This protects you, others, and your relationships from needless harm and suffering.

With "okay," you are saying, "I'm not agreeing or disagreeing with you. I'm listening and allowing." "Okay" communicates giving permission and reflects a loving, wise, and compassionate stance. Practice responding with "okay"—and really meaning it!—and notice the effect this has on you, others, and all of your relationships. You'll be amazed at the difference it makes.

88.
"HEIGHT TURNS TO DEPTH."

Most romances commence with an abundance of passion, excitement, and enthusiasm. When you first encounter a lover, the two of you can't seem to get enough of each other. It's intoxicating, seemingly everything you've ever wanted, and you hungrily celebrate this newfound union.

The initial heights of such romances feel extraordinary, and you want this feeling to last forever. But over time it inevitably fades, and you're likely to assume the relationship is changing for the worse. You miss the early days and wonder how to get those initial feelings back. Many couples come to counseling with this goal. They want to return to the way things were and fear that if they don't, the relationship will end.

In truth, the natural and ideal evolution of a relationship is toward an increase in *depth*. As height wanes, depth grows. This is fantastic! It's exactly what you want, because depth is actually infinitely more extraordinary than height. Unfortunately, few couples arrive at the deepest stage of relationships because, as height turns to depth, the relationship passes through a period that seems mundane, perhaps even boring. Here, many couples decide to part ways, unaware of what is really going on: the relationship is growing in a healthy way.

True intimacy, passion, and love exist in the depths, not the heights. Embracing depth in exchange for height gives permission for your relationships to enter and flourish within this extraordinary domain, growing deeper and deeper over the passing years.

89.
"EMOTIONS ARE LIKE SMOKE DETECTORS."

Many people come to therapy because they don't like the way they're feeling and want it to change. They think their emotional state is the problem—that their emotions need fixing. This is untrue. In reality, nothing is wrong with their emotions. Their emotions are functioning perfectly.

To understand why this is the case, imagine that you're at home and the smoke detector goes off. Immediately, you want the darn thing to stop blaring. Maybe you remove the battery, pound the alarm with your fists, or even rip it off the wall. But if your house is on fire and all you do is try to silence the smoke detector because it's a nuisance, you're going to be in trouble. Attending to the alarm, rather than the fire, wouldn't be a helpful strategy. Oddly enough, this is something that most of us do. We attend to the alarm instead of the fire.

Emotions are like smoke detectors, constantly alerting us to what's arising within ourselves or our circumstances. If these alarms are loud enough, we may try to silence them, thinking that the alarms themselves are the problem, instead of looking at what these alarms are trying to signal to us. When these internal alarms are sounding, there's always a good reason. Somewhere a fire is burning, and if we ignore it, it will grow.

Emotions serve a purpose. They are doing their job, flawlessly, all the time. They're trying to get you to pay attention to something by creating enough discomfort that you'll stop and realize something is amiss, and the bigger this something is, the more adamantly your emotions strive for your attention. Whether that fire is small or large, you can't extinguish it until you find it, and your emotions won't change until you do.

Throughout your life, you'll probably feel many emotions that you don't like or want. Regardless of how much you like or dislike what you're feeling, understand your emotions for what they are: information, and very valuable information at that. Ideally, you'd respond to emotions first by giving yourself permission for feeling as you do. You can even embrace your emotions with a measure of gratitude, knowing that they are trying to help you. Your emotions are your ally, never your enemy.

I can't tell you how often I hear people proclaim, "I hate feeling this way!" Understandable though this sentiment may be, a more beneficial perspective would be "I'm thankful I feel this way," followed by "Now I know just how profoundly things are not the way I want. It's time to do something about this!"

In many ways, suffering is a blessing. Our emotions, no matter how uncomfortable, are trying to inspire us to action and make the changes we desire. Emotions never need fixing, because they are never broken; they are always working perfectly well. Once we recognize this, we can embrace every emotion with wisdom and start creating the life we want for ourselves. Then our emotions will stop clamoring for attention and start celebrating with us instead, because they will have done their job.

90.
"LYING IS OKAY."

When I say, "Lying is okay," I don't intend this statement to be used as a justification for lying to others. Rather, I want to offer an explanation for why others sometimes lie to you. Trust is a big deal, and extraordinary relationships have an abundance of trust. So how can it be that lying is okay?

Trust and lying are closely intertwined, though not in the way you probably think. Lying doesn't undermine trust. It may seem that it does, but this entire book has been about seeing beyond what *appears* to be true so that you can, with compassionate wisdom, embrace what is *actually* true. And when it comes to lying, the truth is that there's nothing wrong with it.

Lying, like everything else, happens for a reason. In childhood we learned that it doesn't always pay to be honest. We discovered this each time a caregiver reacted with anger to something we did or said. We realized that if the truth wasn't to someone's liking, then it was better, for our sake and theirs, to lie. It was the emotional reactions of others that first taught us the merits of dishonesty.

The reality is that people lie because they don't trust that their honesty will be received in a calm and understanding way. And most of the time this is true. So the reason why lying is okay is that it can be viewed as valuable information about the state of trust in a relationship. Being lied to by someone doesn't tell you that you can't trust the person; it tells you that the person doesn't trust you.

When people lie to you, you can get angry at them about it, but what will that achieve? Will they lie less often? Probably not. Paradoxically, they will be more likely to lie because you have confirmed, through your acting out of a state of emotional reaction, their suspicion that you would not genuinely welcome the truth.

Lying doesn't undermine trust; it reflects that trust has already been somehow undermined.

When people lie to you, it's helpful to pause for a moment to examine the extent to which you might have played a role in this, rather than judging their disinclination to be honest. Perhaps in the past you've shown them that you're unwilling or unable to accept honesty without reacting emotionally and acting out. Understand that their history of experiences with you (or sometimes with others) has led them to opt for lying over being honest. Then, rather than faulting them, you can give permission.

If you truly value honesty and want to cultivate trust in your relationships, the way to achieve this is by giving permission and taking responsibility. You build trust by showing others that they can share the truth with you without being punished for doing so.

Can you do anything to help increase others' trust in you? Absolutely. If they feel castigated for being honest, will this help increase their trust in you? Absolutely not. What will? Giving permission, understanding the lie as a symptom of mistrust and fear, and then striving to create a climate in which trust and honesty are fully supported.

91.

"ANGER IS NOT AN EMOTION."

Anger certainly seems like an emotion. We feel anger, just like we feel joy or sadness, so it must be an emotion, right? Nope. And here's why. Think of a baby. Babies are able to giggle in wonder-struck amusement and cry at the top of their lungs. They can experience the entire spectrum of human emotion. What they cannot do, however, is get angry. Why? Because anger is not an emotion.

Anger originates from emotion but is not an emotion itself. It is the bodyguard that leaps to the defense of the vulnerable parts of yourself that are actually sad or wounded. This is not to say that anger is ever artificial, just that it is superficial; it masks a sorrow hidden somewhere beneath it. When people come to therapy for anger management, I understand what they are seeking: an answer to their sadness.

The anger that you or others experience in the present moment may seem like a result of recent events. In truth, this triggered reaction generally stems from a buried sadness unresolved from the past, often your history with similar events in childhood. Long ago, as a child, you reacted purely with sadness—for instance, when you were first teased at school. Now when you feel similarly teased, you get angry. This anger is a defense mechanism, not an emotion.

How can you apply this understanding that anger is not an emotion to your aspirations for extraordinary relationships? By recognizing all anger, your own and that of others, for what it really is: sadness. This is helpful because we generally respond to sadness more compassionately than we do to anger. If someone is angry at you, recognize their sadness and respond accordingly. When you are angry, recognize your own sadness and respond accordingly, with love, tenderness, and care.

92.
"TO TRULY LOVE
IS TO LIKE."

Most people consider love to be "like" amplified. I'd suggest that love isn't a higher form of liking, but that liking is distinct and every bit the equal of love, if not its superior. Let me explain.

The word "love" is nearly impossible to define. It's generally used to describe a strong positive feeling for someone or something. It comes in many forms: romantic love, brotherly love, unconditional love, universal love, spiritual love, true love, and the list goes on. Most people agree that love, in its purest form, is selfless in nature. Many people even suggest that God is love. This is a fine definition, but that isn't the type of love most people experience. As most people define their feelings, love is usually conditional, egoistic, and codependent. As such, it may frequently be accompanied by much suffering and heartache. True love never causes suffering. Ordinary love, in contrast, seems to cause tons of it.

Many unfortunate acts have been committed by those in the throes of what is perceived as love. People can be physically and emotionally abusive toward one another out of love. People can attack and fight one another out of love. People sometimes even murder others out of pain presumably caused by love. And even when love doesn't drive us to such extremes, it can cloud our senses and trigger us to treat others and ourselves destructively because we care so much that we feel out of control.

This seems counterintuitive, so why does it happen? Early in life, most of us learned that our parents or primary caregivers loved us. They said so repeatedly, so this knowledge became ingrained. This wasn't a problem until we began getting scolded. As children, we were extremely sensitive. We didn't enjoy getting reprimanded, and it hurt. If punishments were severe enough, we may have come to fear our parents or caregivers, even though we knew they loved us. We discovered that being loved sometimes comes with a cost, and that it isn't always rewarding or easy to be loved.

Most children know, without a doubt, that their parents or caregivers love them. What they don't know, however, is whether their parents or caregivers *like* them. And this is the question that, as children, we cared about most. Are we liked? That's what we really wanted to know.

Most parents are adept at expressing love toward their children but not so great at expressing that they like them. After all, as children age, they become less compliant, more rebellious, and harder to control, and parents aren't exactly thrilled by this. They don't like having their children talk back or attempt to assert their independence. At times, their dislike shows, and when this happens, children tend to interpret this dislike as directed at them personally, rather than at their behavior. When children consider the possibility that their own parents don't like them, this makes them doubt their inherent likeability, value, and worth. Love is never in question, but liking is, and relationships suffer as a result.

I remember a single mother who brought her teenage daughter in for counseling complaining that her daughter had explosive anger and poor social skills. She was exasperated because she and her daughter fought constantly and her daughter was starting to get into fights at school. In her mind, her daughter needed to improve her attitude and learn to better handle her emotions. When they arrived, I met privately with the daughter first and learned that she thought her mother didn't like her. She showed no signs of anger or aggression toward me. In fact, she was quite calm, polite, respectful, and open with her feelings. We talked a while longer, and then I met individually with the mother, having first gotten consent from the daughter to disclose what she and I had discussed. When I told the mom what her daughter had said, her response, which she said almost proudly, was "Of course I don't like her!" I didn't need to hear another word to diagnose what was going on. The daughter's explosive anger was a reflection of not feeling liked by the primary adult figure in her life, and the worst part was, it was true.

The solution was to work with the mother alone, teaching her, over the course of several months, how to express that she liked her daughter while also focusing on increasing her own happiness. About a year after I stopped working with her, she sent me this note: "I was telling a friend about having therapy with you and how much you were able to help me be a better mom, and I wanted to give you an update. Liddy and I are doing well—really, really well. We talk and laugh, and I get a lot of hugs and kisses from her. I leave the house some evenings to do volunteer work, which gives me a great deal of pleasure and her some alone time, and we actually miss each other. Liddy is growing into a wonderful young lady and is looking forward to high school."

Before therapy, Liddy knew that her mom loved her, but this wasn't enough. She wanted to be liked. It's what we all want, whether we choose to admit this or not. Being liked is pure and uncomplicated. It's refreshingly genuine, revealing itself in simple ways, like when someone smiles at you or lights up when you enter a room. Liking joyfully embraces others as they are and asks little in return. Ordinary love, in contrast, can be demanding, judgmental, and difficult. Liking may not have all of the fireworks of love, but it doesn't have the ills of love either. Like is always beautiful, the way a pebble can be beautiful. No unfortunate act has ever been committed in the name of like.

If you think of love as more important than like, you may forget to spend time liking those you love. Understand that true love cannot exist without liking. The next time you want to tell your partner (or anyone else), "I love you," try saying, "I like you," instead. See how the person responds. See how you feel when sharing this information. Like is, without question, extraordinary.

93.
"EVERYONE IS LIKEABLE."

You have the ability to like anyone. When you refrain from judging others, recognizing that everyone is essentially the same, born innocent at birth and inherently beautiful, and then relate directly to their innate humanness, you can honor and accept others unconditionally, just as they are.

Liking and disliking arise from giving or not giving permission. Since you can always choose to give permission, you can always choose to like. When you embrace your ability to like rather than dislike others, the results are always positive. There is no risk in replacing socially conditioned judgments with wisdom and choosing to like others.

Indeed, liking is a reflection of wisdom—a wisdom defined by giving permission. This wisdom can have profound effects on yourself and others. After all, liking feels better than disliking, and you can bestow this gift on yourself. And being liked feels better than being disliked, and you can bestow this gift on others.

This is no less true when it comes to liking yourself. You can choose to like yourself by giving yourself permission to be who and how you are, sparing yourself unnecessary and harmful self-judgments. When you choose to like yourself, the benefits are doubled. You get to experience the joy of liking and the joy of being liked at the same time. What a phenomenal way to build internal friendship!

94.
"RIGHT NOW, NOTHING IS WRONG."

The truth is, at this very instant, nothing is wrong. Everything in the past has already happened, and everything in the future is unknown and unknowable. Every conflict, every argument or dispute, and every emotional disturbance that you experience occurs while your mind is disconnected from this present moment, a moment that is constantly born anew.

What you experience in the present moment is always just physical sensations. You see, feel, smell, taste, and hear. That's it. When you suffer, whatever you're reacting to is either already in your past, even if only a few milliseconds ago, or in your future: that which has yet to occur, and may never occur. Whatever you see, feel, smell, taste, and hear is just that and nothing more. Reacting to these sensations entails placing meaning, interpretations, and judgments on them. This process may not take long, but it does take time.

When you chase what was, you miss what is. You miss the present moment, which has arisen to replace the one to which you are reacting. It's entirely impossible to emotionally react when your mind is in the present moment. As such, since emotional reactions are synonymous with suffering, you cannot suffer in the present moment—in each new "now." You can suffer only when your mind is in the past or future.

To illustrate this point during counseling, I sometimes ask clients to try a quick exercise. I hand them a ping-pong ball and paddle and ask that they simply bounce the ball up and down for about a minute. Afterward, I ask if they experienced any suffering while doing this. The answer is always no. Why? Because, during that minute, their mind and body were connected and fully engaged in the present moment.

Keeping your attention perpetually in the present moment, without digression, is virtually impossible. Meditators may spend their entire lives attempting to cultivate this ability and still only partially succeed. Therefore, you shouldn't expect yourself to do this. However, it is helpful to recognize that, in the present moment, nothing is ever wrong. If you can connect to the present moment, you will experience the flawlessness of this moment and give yourself a reprieve from the emotional stress that often results from thinking about the past or future.

Go ahead and take a moment to notice yourself. You're here, alive, just being you, exactly as you are, right now. It's nothing special, and yet nothing could be more special than this. Take a moment to really appreciate it. Pause. Pay attention to your breathing for a second. Allow yourself to experience the stillness of connecting with this present moment, just as it is. Connect with yourself, just as you are, without judgment, guilt, shame, or struggle. Here you are, just breathing and being aware that you're breathing. Notice that, in this moment, all is well.

Meditation, practiced properly and somewhat regularly, will cultivate your ability to give permission to everything and everyone, especially to yourself. Nothing has changed my life more. In fact, the very best use of this book might be for you to put it on the floor and start using it as a meditation cushion (although you can certainly find more comfortable roosts). You will learn more from yourself in this way than you could ever possibly learn from me, or from anyone else. Consider giving yourself the gift of such a wonderful and rewarding practice. To get you started, the recommended reading section offers a short list of some of my and Sabrina's favorite books about meditation.

95.
"APPRECIATING THE OCEAN IS EASY."

When you give permission and don't get lost in judgments about good and bad or right and wrong, when you connect to whatever is, exactly as it is, without insistence that things be otherwise, you become genuinely appreciative. And when you appreciate something, you recognize its inherent perfection, flaws and all. You can witness this perfection in anything, yourself and others included. When you pay attention and give permission, you connect to this awareness. This isn't as hard as it might sound.

Imagine going to an isolated beach for no reason other than to relax. You're alone with the sand and the sea and the sky. Everything is quiet save for the sound of the waves and the occasional call of a seagull. The sun shines and a breeze caresses your cheek. You sit down in this serene setting facing the ocean, relaxing without a care in the world. You take it all in.

Perhaps the ocean is calm on this day. You watch the waves gently ebb and flow against the shore, listen to the hushing sound of each wave as it combs across the sand, and think to yourself, "Ah, beautiful." You appreciate the ocean for what it is in the moment: undulating, tame, and peaceful. You experience its magnificence, just as it is.

Perhaps, on another day, you arrive to find the ocean turbulent rather than calm. You sit down and relax, taking it all in. As the waves soar up and crash down, you listen to the thundering break of each, watch the vibrant explosions of salty mist and spray, and marvel at the impressive force of the ocean. You think to yourself, "Ah, beautiful." Again, you appreciate the ocean for what it is in the moment: tempestuous, dynamic, full of energy and power. You experience its magnificence, just as it is.

In either case, you don't wish the ocean were different. You accept it easily, appreciating it in whatever state it happens to be in. The ocean is always just being the ocean: sometimes calm, sometimes turbulent, other times in between. You understand that the ocean itself isn't responsible for being calm or not, that it's influenced by innumerable factors: the moon and the tide, currents and weather patterns, the shape of the coastline, and so much more. Since you understand that the ocean isn't at fault for its current state, you give it permission to be what it is. Whether it's calm, turbulent, or somewhere in between, you appreciate the ocean all the same. You appreciate its inherent magnificence.

Sitting across from another person need not be any different than this. The nature of the ocean changes, and that's okay. The nature of humans changes, and that's okay too. You can appreciate it all. You can sit and observe someone in a given moment, just as you would the ocean, and think to yourself, "Ah, beautiful." You can meet, embrace, respect, accept, and appreciate others exactly as they are, however they are, whenever you encounter them. However they are is always just fine.

You can always appreciate that someone is beautiful. This isn't a judgment; it's a recognition. Everyone *is* beautiful, just as they are, in every moment. This is the wisdom that exists at the heart of giving permission. When you stay true to this wisdom, knowing that everyone is beautiful and perfect—imperfections and all—then giving permission is natural and effortless. With wisdom, you understand that everyone is beautiful, the way a piece of grass or a park bench or a rainstorm is beautiful—and so are you.

96.
"EMBRACE WHAT IS."

Right now, you are who you are and your life is what it is. Right now, everyone you know is exactly as they are and your relationships with them are exactly as they are. As such, you have a choice. You can fight against what is, struggling for change, or you can give permission for things to be exactly as they are right now. You can suffer, or you can embrace.

Here's a thought exercise I occasionally employ with clients, most often with those whose thinking is dominated by complaints and negativity about themselves and their circumstances. It goes like this: Imagine that, magically, you could automatically become someone else living on the planet right now. The only caveat is that there's no predicting who this will be. When I ask clients if they'd want to swap places with someone at random, they inevitably say, "No way!"

Why? If they are suffering so much unhappiness and discontent, if they have so many complaints and dissatisfactions, why don't they want to trade it all in? Because part of them recognizes that, in truth, there is much in their lives for which they are thankful. While we humans have an unfortunate tendency to fixate on what we don't like about ourselves, our lives, and our relationships, we still recognize that there is much that we do like and value. On a deep level, we all know this; we just occasionally forget.

Your life is as it is, and you have your own unique forms of imperfection in your life. You will never live completely free of difficulties, stress, and suffering. Understanding this, you might as well give permission to yourself to have the life that you have.

When you want yourself or your life to be different, you probably aren't embracing what is, exactly as it is. It may be helpful to remember the parable of the genie who can bestow whatever you desire. When you make your first wish, it is granted immediately.

Let's say you ask to be in love. Voilà! Wish granted! You suddenly find yourself in love, kneeling on the ground with your beloved, recently deceased, in your arms.

"Wait!" you exclaim. "That's not what I wanted."

You try again, this time wishing for immense wealth. Voilà! Wish granted! You suddenly find yourself alone, locked in a vault that's filled with cash but has no exit.

"Wait! This wasn't what I wanted either!"

Whatever wish you ask to have granted, the genie always throws in a catch. Eventually, if you are wise, you realize the one wish you truly want granted: "I wish to have no more wishes." The genie smiles knowingly at you, proud as can be, and then moves on to his next pupil.

This is, indeed, what all of us want: to have no more wishes. We want to know how to embrace our lives for what they are, just as they are. Why? Because life is good enough, just as it is. This is true not only of our lives, but of ourselves as well. Who you are, right now, exactly as you are, is okay; it's good enough. And, just like you, everyone else is good enough too. Recognizing this, you can give permission and reap all the rewards of doing so. You can embrace what is. As you seek changes in yourself, your life, and your relationships, recognize that you can embrace each moment throughout this process. Don't be so concerned about improvement that you miss each perfection along the way. Each step of our journey is equally precious and equally worth our embrace.

97.
"HAPPINESS IS NOT THE GOAL."

What do you want? To be happy? Of course! But, here's the thing: You can't be happy all the time. Why? Because you are human and, as such, blessed with the ability to experience a rich spectrum of emotions. Happiness is only one of the gifts life has to offer. Do you really want to miss out on all the others?

If you seek happiness exclusively, you aren't giving yourself permission to experience everything that life has to offer. Give yourself permission to be sad when sad, happy when happy, bored when bored, annoyed when annoyed, and so on, all without judgment. Give this permission to others, as well. Whenever you give permission, suffering transforms. In truth, the goal isn't to be happy, but to be free from suffering, and therefore the goal is this: to be extraordinary at giving permission, to be able to embrace all our emotions as they arise, and to take responsibility for what we do with them next.

By giving permission, you can let go of the struggle and embrace the wisdom that frees you to love both yourself and others without suffering. You can allow all of your emotions. When you do this, you'll find yourself smiling, because there will be no reason whatsoever not to smile. You will be smiling not necessarily because you're happy, but because you are giving permission and taking responsibility.

98.
"You don't have to order from the menu."

When at a restaurant, most of us order from the menu. We examine the options and then select what looks best. This is also how we tend to approach our lives. We look at the options that are obvious and then select among them. But items on a menu are always limited—perhaps half a dozen appetizers, twice as many entrées, and some desserts. If you go to the same restaurant often, you're bound to get tired of eating there. Here's the thing: Your life is a restaurant you go to every single day. If you keep ordering from the same menu, you're probably going to fall into a routine and get bored.

Routine isn't inherently boring. If you cultivate an ability to be mindful of your experience, you can joyfully move rocks around all day. Realistically speaking, though, few of us have cultivated this ability. Most of us live fairly normal lives that have become a bit repetitive. Many of my clients say things like "I feel like I'm stuck in a rut." Well, most of us *are* stuck in a rut. Why? Because we order from the same menu day in, day out.

What I mean by "ordering from the menu" is choosing only from the options you readily see before you. When you get some free time and consider what to do, you scan your brain for the things you usually do (reading, taking the dog out, watching television, going to see a movie), then choose among those options. When considering approaching your partner about an issue that's bothering you, you choose among the options that are your norm (criticize, demand, get self-righteous, withdraw, or unsuccessfully try to avoid the issue). You order from the menu. This menu is in your brain, written by your previous experiences.

Since we generally only consider things we've done in the past as options, it makes perfect sense that our lives become routine. Doesn't it seem like you've been doing much the same thing year after year? This is what happens when you keep ordering off a menu that hasn't changed much over the years.

Children don't order from the menu. They explore their surroundings with unbridled curiosity and abandon. They go wherever their fancy takes them. To children, life is full of new experiences, and each new experience shapes who they become. And the more new experiences we have, the more we change. This is why children change so rapidly: because so much of their experience is brand-new to them. They're still designing their menu.

As adults, most of us have written our menus. In fact, our menus are practically chiseled into our ganglia. If we continually order from this menu, we have fewer new experiences and our growth slows. But guess what? You aren't obligated to order from the menu! You can ask the kitchen to prepare anything you want. You can fully embrace the enormity of your freedom—a freedom limited only by your imagination.

A quick story: One of my clients read the manuscript for this book and told me that this chapter was one of his favorites. Where is he now? I honestly can't tell you. Inspired by the message of this chapter, he made arrangements with his employer to work remotely, sold off most of his possessions, hopped into his car, and took to the road to travel wherever his path takes him. I don't know where he is right now, but I do know that, wherever he is, he's ordering something not on the menu.

99.
"YOU ARE THE ONLY ONE WHO GETS TO BE YOU."

There is no one exactly like you. No one sees the world as you do, thinks the way you think, or feels like you feel. You are unique—a one-of-a-kind specimen. Even if you suffer, it is *your* suffering. If you are happy or sad, that is *your* happiness or sadness. If you love, that's *your* love and no one else's. Here you are, right now, reading these words and taking them in as only you can.

This is your most rare of privileges: being the only person on the planet who gets to know, fully and truly, what it's like to be you. This makes you extremely special, and extremely lucky.

To cultivate an extraordinary life with extraordinary relationships, start by honoring yourself for being who you are, exactly as you are. The more you do so, the more you'll be able to honor others for being who they are. As you respect your own uniqueness as beautiful, imperfections and all, you'll be better able to respect the uniqueness of others as beautiful too.

At the risk of sounding corny, Sabrina and I want to take this opportunity to say that we have never met a client we didn't perceive as loveable. We love each and every one of our past and current clients because we know that loving means embracing people completely for who they are, and for how they might change along the way. We love because we see no reason not to. We love because we understand that we're allowed to—that it's our choice to make. And why do we make that choice? Because it feels better to love than to judge. You can make this choice too. You can choose to love yourself and others. All it takes is giving permission. When you forgo judgments and simply witness another, the truth of who this person is emerges. And when this happens, love appears.

I once worked with a woman with low-self esteem who was in marriage counseling with her husband. Her husband was absolutely smitten with her, but she couldn't see it. She let her poor self-image color her perception of her husband's affection and refused to believe that he loved her as much as he claimed. As a homework assignment, I asked her to tell herself repeatedly, as sort of a mantra, "It is inarguably true that I am loveable."

At first she scoffed at my suggestion, and then she smiled. Actually, her entire being seemed to light up as her eyes welled with tears. It was as if this one pronouncement reminded her of something she had known all along but had forgotten. After all, I was only sharing the facts with her; I wasn't being metaphysical in the least. I knew she was loveable because, regardless of how she felt about herself, her husband obviously loved her. And, since he loved her, this literally proved that she was loveable—capable of being loved. This is true of everyone. Everyone is capable of being loved and is therefore loveable.

As this book draws to a close, take a moment to recognize this simple truth, repeating the following expression of wisdom to yourself: "It is inarguably true that I am loveable." It's true. You are loveable—so loveable that I don't want to stop writing this book for you! But alas, we are almost finished here. There's just one more thing to cover: your homework.

100.
"HAVE FUN!"

In childhood, when you wanted to build forts out of sofa cushions, you built forts out of sofa cushions. When you wanted to paint or draw pictures, you painted or drew pictures. When you wanted to wear costumes and pretend you were a pirate or princess, you wore costumes and pretended you were a pirate or princess. You did these things because you wanted to, because you gave yourself permission to do just that. That was total authenticity, total liberty, and total bliss.

Life is too short (and too long) to not have fun. Sure, as an adult you have responsibilities you didn't have in childhood. But your responsibilities don't preclude you from having fun. I'd go so far as to suggest that, in fact, your biggest responsibility is to have fun. Why? Because if you aren't having fun, then you aren't being truly authentic, and you aren't giving yourself permission. If you don't give yourself permission, how can you be joyful? And if you aren't joyful, how can you share joyfulness with others? And if you can't share joyfulness with others, then what's the purpose of being responsible? Fun is about giving yourself permission to live a genuinely fulfilling life. You deserve this.

Fun is the polestar that can guide you toward the life you want to be living—a life of joyfulness, fulfillment, and extraordinary relationships. Let yourself be guided. Let yourself follow what's fun for you. What you find fun comes from a deep place within you. When you give yourself permission to have fun, you give yourself permission to live your life in fulfillment every day. Decide to be joyful and have fun. Cultivate loving and meaningful relationships because doing so is fun. Embrace yourself, your life, and others because doing so is fun.

Have fun and you will prosper. Have fun and your relationships will prosper. There's nothing irresponsible or selfish about this. In fact, I firmly believe that having fun ultimately leads not toward greater selfishness, but to a life spent in the service of others. How? Because giving to others, making a positive difference in their lives, is a genuinely joyful—and fun—experience.

This book has been not only about loving and helping yourself; it has been about knowing that loving and helping yourself is how you can best love and help others. When you give permission and take responsibility, your life, your relationships, and the entire world will benefit.

An extraordinary life is one filled with extraordinary relationships, internal and external alike. Cultivating such relationships need not be difficult or arduous. It can be fun. So I will assign you some homework, the same homework I give to clients most often: Have fun. I assign this to you in parting because I know this is exactly what you deserve. You deserve to have fun. The world deserves for you to have fun too. In a sense, this is exactly what this entire book has been about: how to start having fun—the genuine, meaningful fun that comes from giving permission and taking responsibility. Do it for your sake, for the sake of those in your life, those you have yet to encounter, and even for those you will never meet. The kind of fun that inspires extraordinary relationships has an amazing way of becoming contagious.

So please, have fun appreciating everything life is offering you, in this very moment and in each moment onward. Have fun embracing others and everything they have to offer you, right now and in the future. Have fun living in the extraordinary way that comes from giving permission and taking responsibility. Have fun creating an abundance of truly extraordinary relationships.

EPILOGUE

I take little credit for what is written in this book. Truthfully, I feel humbled to have been given the opportunity to learn what I have learned during my years as a therapist. Credit goes to my clients for being such generous teachers. And as humbled as I am to have had them share these lessons with me, I am humbled even more by having the privilege to pass along their lessons. I am both humbled and grateful, in ways that words cannot convey.

My gratitude stems from an immense sense of hope I have for the future, not my own future or even yours, although you are an indispensable part of this. My hope is for all humanity. My hope is that, through the art of giving permission and wisdom of taking responsibility, the way all humans relate to one another will change. This transformation would open the door to peace on earth and an end to suffering and senseless conflict.

I realize this is an expansive hope, but I am unwilling to believe it is impossible or unrealistic. I trust that this possibility exists, that worldwide peace is achievable. In fact, I even trust it is inevitable. Whether it takes a hundred years or a thousand, I trust that the truths of giving permission and taking responsibility will ultimately become so ordinary that there will be nothing extraordinary about them. They will simply be the way everyone lives—the way everyone treats themselves and others.

Simply writing this book was not my and Sabrina's goal; it is a means to an end, not an end in itself. As such, we have yet to succeed, because we can do only so much on our own. Changing the way all humans view and participate in relationships—well, this is obviously not something we can accomplish alone. Indeed, we could use some help, and we invite your assistance in realizing this vision for a better world.

How can you help? You can transform yourself and your own relationships, each and every one of them, toward the extraordinary. Then, when others experience your joyfulness and ask what accounts for it, you can inform them about giving permission and taking responsibility. Perhaps they will view this as an opportunity to cultivate their own extraordinary relationships, spreading the gift of these truths to more and more people.

As we pass the two truths on and on in this way, at some time in the future all children may be born into a world free from interpersonal suffering, hatred, struggle, and war—a world in which everyone willingly and skillfully shares extraordinary relationships with one another, a world where giving permission and taking responsibility is commonplace, a world guided by love, compassion, and wisdom. No matter how long this takes, it will be worth it.

Please help us. We cannot do this on our own.

Please help everyone, those living now and those yet to be born.

Together, we can do this. We can replace suffering with joyfulness, warmth, and understanding.

Together, we can gently lead the way toward harmony and intimacy.

Together, we can inspire the entire world, one extraordinary relationship at a time.

Know that our greatest prayer is this: may you live an extraordinary life and share that life with others.

RECOMMENDED READING

The following books may be immensely helpful in cultivating a practice of meditation and mindfulness:

- *Zen Mind, Beginner's Mind*, by Shunryu Suzuki Roshi

- *Mindfulness in Plain English*, by Bhante Henepola Gunaratana

- *Peace Is Every Step*, by Thich Nhat Hanh

- *Comfortable with Uncertainty*, by Pema Chödrön

- *A Path with Heart*, by Jack Kornfield

- *The Contemplative Heart*, by James Finley

The Two Truths About Love is only a map. It's the steps you take in the future, guided by this map, that make all the difference. As such, this book is only a beginning. To continue your ongoing journey toward extraordinary relationships, you can find additional writings, as well as Jason's free instructional video on zazen meditation, online at www.jasonbfischer.com.

Lastly, Jason and Sabrina want to offer their wholehearted support to help you fully realize the principles of this exciting approach to life and love. As such, they look forward to you joining them at one of their workshops or retreats. If you take advantage of the opportunity to delve deeply into this life-changing philosophy by working with them directly, you'll discover just how extraordinary your life can be. To get started, you'll find a schedule of upcoming events, along with other resources and videos, online at www.theartofgivingpermission.com

 **Jason B. Fischer, MA, LPC,** is a licensed psychotherapist who has a thriving counseling practice in Austin, TX. He is the clinical director and owner of Plumeria Counseling Center, which he founded with the underlying mission of providing quality, affordable counseling to all those who desire it. He additionally spent time as a fully ordained Theravadin Buddhist monk, before reentering conventional society to "walk the middle path." His lifelong ambition is to help foster a global community free from suffering and interpersonal disharmony.

 **Sabrina Kindell, MA, LPC, LMFT,** is a dual-licensed marriage and family therapist and professional counseling supervisor. She specializes in family dynamics, parenting, and partnering. She has been in an extraordinary relationship with her husband for over twenty-five years and has two grown children.

MORE BOOKS *from*
NEW HARBINGER PUBLICATIONS

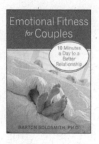

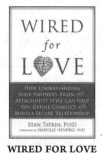